HONORING YOUR SELF

The Promise
of the Twelve Steps

A divine welcome

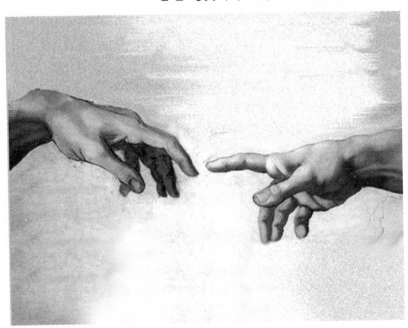

awaits your reach…

HONORING *your Self*

A Guide to Overcoming Addictions

HOB

Recovery Bound Publications Ltd.
Carson City, Nevada

Published by:
Recovery Bound Publications Ltd.
711 South Carson Street, Suite 4
Carson City, NV 89701

Editors: Ellen Kleiner, John Nelson
Book design and production: Janice St. Marie
Front cover image: Josef
Cover art: Christinea Johnson
Cover design: Jody Dark Eagle Breedlove

A Blessingway book

Printed in the United States of America on acid-free recycled paper

Publisher's Cataloging-in-Publication Data

Hob.
    Honoring your self : a guide to overcoming addictions / Hob. —
1st ed.
    p. cm.
    LCCN: 99-74086
    ISBN: 0-9671557-8-9

    1. Addicts—Rehabilitation. 2. Twelve-step programs. 3. Substance
abuse—Treatment. 4. Psychology, Pathological I. Title

HV4998.H63 2000   616.86'06
                                                QB199-885

10 9 8 7 6 5 4 3 2 1

To all kindred spirits, with love

In Gratitude...

What a wonderful team effort this has been, thanks to my lovely wife
Kairina and to Ellen Kleiner, editor extraordinaire; John Nelson,
developmental wizard; Janice St. Marie; Josef; Christinea Johnson;
Jody Dark Eagle Breedlove; the recovering addicts who agreed to
share their stories; and above all, Alcoholics Anonymous cofounders
Bill W. and Dr. Bob.

Contents

Preface

My name is Hob, and I'm an alcoholic. Although some people are born alcoholics, I became one. Like a leaf blown hither and thither in the wind, I drifted into the insidious grip of drinking.

I grew up in Ohio, as the middle child in a family of nine. My family belonged to the social register; we can trace our heritage directly back to the Mayflower. My parents were religious and did not drink. Dad served as a deacon in the church where we children attended Sunday school. There my favorite song was "Jesus Loves Me," whose words I still remember.

I have a strong bond with my father. He saved my life when he noticed me lying facedown in my crib and turning blue. Dad rolled me over and sent out a prayer, at which point I began to breathe again. As a young child, I would trudge around the house in his hobnailed boots, which eventually earned me the nickname "Hob." When I was ten, Dad died of leukemia. I was devastated and felt betrayed. This memory still brings tears to my eyes. It was many years later that I finally forgave him. He was my closest friend—and still is.

The following year I attended summer camp. The director, whom I considered a surrogate father, tried to sexually molest me. Having grown up in a religious family, I was naive about such matters. When I reported the incident, he was fired. This was another betrayal of trust, and it had a devastating effect on me. Shortly afterward, my eyesight began to seriously deteriorate.

I was still recovering from the loss of my father when I joined my two older brothers at a fashionable prep school. While they excelled as students, I had a trouble focusing on my studies. My difficulties were somewhat mitigated by my sports triumphs. I played basketball, earned a letter in track, and was the youngest student in the school's history to letter in baseball. It was at age sixteen, while going out with older members of the baseball team, that I drank my first beer, and I didn't at all like the taste of it. Aside from sports and having fun with team members, I was forever getting into trouble—setting off chapel clocks, climbing water towers, and breaking all sorts of rules. As a result of my pranks, I eventually lost my scholarship and ended up at a public high school.

Throughout my school years, I was an avid reader. One essay that struck a chord was Ralph Waldo Emerson's "Self-Reliance," which I read at the age of fifteen. It reminded me that when all else failed I could count on myself. Another significant school experience came when my roommate and I started what I now call "inspired writing." We would turn down the light, then recite Mary Baker Eddy's words: "There's no life, truth, intelligence, or substance in matter. All is infinite mind and its infinite manifestations, for God is all in all." After that, we began to write—he more quickly than I, for my hands would shake uncontrollably from all the energy passing through them.

One day while writing, we both received a very nice message that was signed "A. Conan Doyle." We looked at each other and asked, "Who's A. Conan Doyle?" Although we would later learn about Sherlock Holmes's creator, already I knew that this writing had become a means for expressing everything within me. These clandestine adventures in communication with the dead revealed a realm beyond the world of the five senses that I would explore further someday. When I showed the writings to my mother, she quickly sent me to our minister, who advised me to forget about them until I was older. So I did.

After high school, my life took a course unlike those of my siblings, who all went to college. My two brothers graduated from Yale, and my sisters received degrees from Oberlin and Wooster. But I needed to discover life my own way—through direct experience and through reading. So I took a job as a common laborer in a steel mill.

One day, instead of going to work I chugged off for the West Coast in my old Packard. There I boarded a ship bound for Hawaii and later that night gave myself up as a stowaway. Earlier, I had told my wealthy uncle in San Francisco to ignore any communication from me, so when the captain sent him a wire, he ignored it. I, meanwhile, was placed in the brig and stayed there until we reached Honolulu, where I spent twenty-five days in jail working off the fine.

While in jail, I was accidentally placed in solitary confinement, which they called "hobo," for three days. Years later, after many drinking binges, I looked back on this experience and realized that I felt freer in solitary than I ever had while drinking. In fact, one of my most powerful arguments for sobriety is that drinking robs me of my precious freedom.

I remained in Hawaii for a year, selling Fuller brushes and doing odd jobs. I was too broke for any serious drinking. And then I was hired as one of five crew members on a forty footer sailing to San Diego. The trip, which lasted thirty-three days, was quite arduous. First, we ran out of food. Then, during a storm I was tossed into the sea while fixing the jib. Fortunately, I grabbed a rope that had washed over, and pulled myself back on board. The crew gave me a slug of Black and White Scotch, and on we sailed—missing our landfall by more than 100 miles. I was a virgin when it came to drinking scotch whiskey, so I remember this first encounter very well! I drank the scotch like a toddler would devour an ice cream cone awarded to him for keeping his pants dry.

At age twenty-two, I returned to the Midwest and immediately fell in love with an exciting and wealthy young woman. Her behavior, however, was quite strange. On the night I gave her a diamond engagement ring and we went to the Yale Ball to celebrate, she didn't return home until 6:00 A.M.—and with her was another man! Soon afterward, she corralled three suitors into her living room, each one sure that he had the inside track. As one of the group, I rolled the dice and asked her, "Just who do you intend to marry?" She snorted like a mare in heat and replied, "I intend to marry truth and beauty. Who's ready for another drink?" I ignored these early warning signs and, much to the dismay of her social-register family, we later eloped.

Sometime before our escape, I took a job at a forge shop, where I became a hammersmith in charge of operating a 5,000-pound steam hammer. I headed up a work gang of five older men. During this period, Great Britain was at war with Germany, and our job was to make crankshafts, landing gears, and torpedo rings for British aircraft and naval vessels. After work, I would wander over to Emery's, the local bar, to have a few beers—and on Fridays to cash my payroll check. Then I headed home for more drinks with my wife-to-be, whose behavior was becoming increasingly bizarre and irresponsible. At first I didn't worry, figuring that she was a free spirit. As for me, despite heavy drinking, I was not yet an alcoholic; I could stop at any time.

One day soon after she and I were married, I had a major disagreement with my boss about our productivity, which I had managed to double. He promptly changed my work status, making me eligible for the draft. Instead of waiting for the Army to draft me, I joined the Marines and said good-bye to my bride. At that point, World War II was in high gear. After boot camp I was sent to the South Pacific, where I remained for nearly three years. I saw action in the Solomon Islands and Guam, gradually working my way up the ranks to platoon sergeant. And during the lulls in fighting, I dreamed about being a writer. In time, I produced a little newsletter, and even started a novel about my experiences in the steel mills.

I returned from the war to discover that my wife was drinking heavily all the time. At last I understood the cause of her strange behavior. But I knew nothing about alcoholism; I simply thought she drank too much. We moved from Greenwich, Connecticut, to New York City, where I found an exciting job as a copywriter with a top advertising agency. After work each day, I would drink extra-dry martinis, as was the protocol. Then I would come home, and my wife and I would settle down to some serious drinking. Although my career in advertising was a great success, I was drinking heavily, beginning at lunch—a two-hour repast. After discovering that martinis had built-in boxing gloves, I switched to vodka. I assumed that everybody drank, and that something was wrong with those who didn't. Eagerly awaiting my first afternoon drink, I was extremely creative in the mornings. And although drinking and working had become a balancing act for me, I was never a falling-down drunk.

By 1950, I had quit my advertising job and joined the United World Federalists' effort to strengthen the United Nations, in the hope of preventing future wars. While working on the Writer's Board for World Government with Oscar Hammerstein, Norman Cousins, John Hershey, and others, I founded the magazine *One World or None* and coined the phrase "Peace is a fighting word"—a slogan that soon appeared in *The New York Times* and *The Washington Post*, as well as on banners throughout the nation.

In 1953, my wife and I moved back to the Greenwich area, and it was there that I attended my first Alcoholics Anonymous (AA) meeting. I knew I was drinking too heavily, and that my wife and I had created our own version of the film *Days of Wine and Roses:* Days of Whine and Neurosis. A meeting, I had figured, might help me slow down. The fellow who took me there worked on Wall Street, and to my amazement the main speaker was the bank executive who had approved the mortgage on our home. Before he told his story, his wife presented him with a cake with five candles, in honor of his fifth anniversary in AA. Everybody in the room cheered.

Looking around, I liked the people I saw. Their faces glowed with what we in the Marine Corps had called the "2,000-yard stare"—a long, beautiful look of serenity. However, despite its appeal, I did not attend another AA meeting. After all, I wasn't an alcoholic, just an "enthusiastic drinker" who had to be more watchful. Shortly afterward, I developed a set of drinking rules: "Don't drink on an empty stomach," "Don't chug-a-lug," and similar cautionary guidelines.

My next career move was to public relations. As assistant to the president of a leading PR firm, I performed my duties well despite a growing dependence on alcohol. Three years later, I was laid off for budgetary reasons and then took a job selling advertising for a science magazine. As a bonus, the president of the company promised me a bottle of Jack Daniel's Black Label for every prominent client I signed on. That was all the incentive I needed. In no time at all, I was handily walking—or should I say, staggering—away with my prized bottles of booze.

I proceeded to drink my way down from selling advertising for a prestigious national publication to peddling Kirby vacuum cleaners door-to-door. Meanwhile, I was becoming frustrated with my inability to stay sober for more than three months at a time. Although I never had a blackout, I did have brownouts (in which you remember what you're doing although the details are a bit fuzzy). Increasingly, when faced with the choice between the bottle and the job, I chose drinking. Booze had soon become my only boss.

As my downward spiral continued, we left the East Coast and returned home to Ohio to live with my mother-in-law. By then, my wife and I had three children, and our drinking problems had worsened. You could compare my binges to Ravel's *Bolero,* which starts out softly and gains momentum until its grand finale—a resounding crash. Once, while angry and hung-over, I blamed my mother-in-law for my wife's alcoholism. Walking away from this confrontation, I happened to glance at a mirror, where I saw the face of a man with a problem: my eyes were glassy and my skin was flushed. I looked terrible. (I would encourage anyone with a drinking problem to be prepared before looking at themselves in a mirror!)

My irate mother-in-law kicked me out of her house. Taking an apartment, I began to live alone. I attended a few more AA meetings as an observer, but I continued to drink. What is the primary difference, I would ask myself, between me and those who have managed to stop drinking? Do they have more willpower than I? Whatever it was they were running on, I wanted it, too.

A month later, while walking away from yet another job failure, I had a talk with myself: "Hob, you notice when your windshield wiper doesn't work, or that you have a hole in your shoe, or are wearing only one glove. Why can't you admit that you're an alcoholic?" I couldn't answer my own question.

That night I needed to talk to somebody, so I called my wife and asked her to meet me at a hotel. Apparently, she didn't detect the urgency in my voice, and never showed up. Desperately needing to talk to someone, I phoned an old Marine Corps buddy in San Diego. After chatting with him for a few minutes and realizing he wasn't hearing my silent shouts for help, I hung up the phone and sat on the bed. From the radio came the soft strains of Tennessee Ernie Ford singing, "Oh, he walks with me, he talks with me, he tells me I am his own." I recognized these lines from "In the Garden," which had been my grandmother's favorite hymn and mine too. I slid off the bed, got down on my knees, and prayed. As a stiff-necked Presbyterian, I had no clue about how to kneel down in prayer or what to say to God. Nevertheless, there I was, praying—first on one side of the bed and then on the other. When I finished, I felt lighter and sensed that I had made contact with an old friend.

Two days later, I walked into Rosary Hall, an AA rehab center in my hometown. There I was greeted by Sister Ignatia, one of AA's original participants, who asked if I was an alcoholic. My mind reeled. I had long considered myself "not very wise" when it came to booze, or someone who "drank the wrong things." She repeated her question: "Are you an alcoholic?"

The man sitting with us, who was to become my temporary sponsor, kicked me under the table, letting me know that to gain entrance I had to admit that I was an alcoholic. I whispered, "Yes, I am," conceding for the first time that I was indeed an alcoholic. This step is the "crossing of the Rubicon" in every recovering alcoholic's life. Why? Because in admitting to alcoholism, you are at once revealing a painful secret to yourself and committing to the journey of recovery. I spent seven days at Rosary Hall, the most they allowed. And then, by the grace of God, I began my life over again—sober. As I left, Sister Ignatia gave me a sacred medallion and told me to send it back if I ever had another drink. I still have it, and I sense that now, from beyond the grave, she continues to applaud my sobriety.

I returned home to the house I then shared with my wife and children, quickly got a job, and began to attend AA meetings on a regular basis. After I had gone to at least three meetings a week for five months, the chairman of my home group asked me to lead a meeting. I was terrified. In a daze I stepped up to the podium, stood there quaking, and poured out my story for fifty-five minutes. When it was over, I felt somehow unburdened. The chairman congratulated me, and said he was placing me on the AA talk circuit. This was high praise from an old pro! Before long, my story was well-known around town.

My loving wife, meanwhile, continued to drink. Although it was difficult to stay sober in her presence, I somehow succeeded. After three years of desperately trying to convince her to join Alcoholics Anonymous, I gave her an HOB ultimatum: "'Hob or Booze'—you have to choose." She chose the latter, and we had a teary farewell. After moving out, I divorced her, leaving our three precious children in her care. Tim was sixteen years old; Laura was fourteen; and Susan, twelve, was two years older than I when I lost my father. Parting ways with my children made the divorce even more difficult. I still remember receiving a letter from Susan telling me, "Mom isn't going to change. You can come home now, Daddy." But I was determined to stay sober at all costs, and could not be around people who weren't. My wife, as it turned out, eventually died of alcoholism.

In the ensuing years, I married and divorced several women. After divorcing my third wife, I lived with a woman who ended up beating me to the escape hatch, which was a blow to my male ego. I remember pacing the floor for hours one night, mumbling to myself, "Poor Hob, you've been jilted." Unable to see rejection as part of the emotional ups and downs of life, I took it very personally. After about three months of hell, I reached for a pen and, quite unexpectedly, began my inspired writing again, picking up where I had left off in prep school. The thoughts just poured out of me, yet now they were about overcoming addiction as well as about spiritual truths.

I am currently living with my fifth wife, Kairina, and we are preparing to celebrate our twenty-first wedding anniversary. My children, now grown, have not escaped the ravages of their parents' alcoholism. Tim, the oldest, came through the ashes of drugs as a teenager, recovering and then thriving at Day Top Village in Staten Island, New York. He was appointed director of a satellite unit in New Hampshire, only to relapse into drugs and alcohol. Hitting a bottom in Los Angeles, he found his Higher Power, and now, seventeen years sober, he works with the alcoholic and mentally disabled in Oregon. He recently married an attorney who has her five-year AA sobriety chip.

My middle child Laura, who lives with her husband and their four children, does birthing and missionary work in Florida. Susan, my youngest, is a recovered dual-addiction RN and the mother of three, one now in AA. The children and I have remained close and deeply loving all these years.

I, meanwhile, continue to write. While under the influence of alcohol, I could not hear my inner voice; now, having walked the path of sobriety, I am able not only to hear it but also to honor it in many ways. *Honoring Your Self* comes from years of listening to words bubbling up from the core of my being. In sobriety, I have attended meetings all over the country, sponsoring and helping others as I have been helped, working to maintain our precious sobriety no matter what life brings us. We recover lost pieces of ourselves a day at a time, and so far it has worked, thank God.

Introduction

Recovery from any addiction is a spiritual journey. More often than not, it begins when we have exhausted all other possibilities, from going cold turkey to submitting to electroshock therapy. Nobody, and certainly not an addict, wants to admit that they are powerless, that no amount of willpower, gumption, intelligence, or technology can on its own vanquish their dependency. And yet, that is what we invariably discover, for addiction is basically a spiritual malaise—or, according to a German translation of the word, the search of the soul to awaken. The only lasting solution is therefore to surrender to a power greater than ourselves.

The idea of an all-knowing, all-powerful spiritual force insults many people who have turned their backs on religion and made a god of ambition, family comfort, good citizenry, or social responsibility. That is why recovery movements use the term "Higher Power *as you know it.*" They address the God in each of us, as we define it. Hence, the spiritual path translates not into regular church attendance but into communion with ourselves, others, and the God in everything. Indeed, for numerous sojourners, as you will see, recovery becomes a quest for the highest and deepest parts of the self that their addiction has cut off.

However, full recovery requires more than surrender: it calls for common sense, courage, humility, fortitude, self-love, and the patience to tackle one day at a time. We must live in the present, releasing old pains and recriminations, and maintaining vigilance every wakeful moment. American Indian shamans are instructed to treat death as their constant companion—an ally who looks over their shoulder and tells them not to "sweat the small stuff." Similarily, our addiction looks over our shoulders, watching and waiting for anger, disappointment, humiliation, or arrogance to open the hatch so it can slide back into our lives.

For example, my first sponsor in AA decided that his body, after seven years of sobriety, had undergone such a thorough chemical alteration that he was no longer an alcoholic. He concluded that he could have two drinks a day without causing harm and without exceeding his quota. The experiment lasted about three months before he slipped into anger and went on a bender. Going back to AA meetings turned out to be a tough assignment. He drifted in and out of the program, then he got drunk at home one night, fell down the stairs, broke his neck, and died. The journey to sobriety is a true test of character: *you either cultivate the traits that take you there—and keep you there—or you invite addiction back into your life.*

I have seen people in recovery go through the most extraordinary transformations: mainliners no longer giving up their children for a fix, but working two jobs to put them through college; mean drunks becoming big brothers; self-proclaimed losers turning into successful businesspeople. Each and every one of these individuals had the courage and humility to admit their powerlessness over their addiction, seek the help of their Higher Power, and work day after day to honor their commitment to sobriety. It is these men and women, rather than today's celebrated film or sports stars, who are my heroes.

Despite the vast differences in the journeys of recovering addicts, the ingredients fueling them are the same: variations on the *Twelve Steps* "chanced upon" by Bill W. and Dr. Bob in Akron, Ohio, in 1935, thus setting the foundation stone for Alcoholics Anonymous, and *ongoing meetings* with a group of like-minded people who are struggling to break free of the poisonous claws of addiction. The Twelve Steps of Alcoholics Anonymous are as follows:

1. We admitted we were powerless over alcohol—that our lives had become unmanageable.

2. Came to believe that a Power greater than ourselves could restore us to sanity.

3. Made a decision to turn our will and our lives over to the care of God *as we understood Him.*

4. Made a searching and fearless moral inventory of ourselves.

5. Admitted to God, to ourselves, and to another human being the exact nature of our wrongs.

6. Were entirely ready to have God remove all these defects of character.

7. Humbly asked Him to remove our shortcomings.

8. Made a list of all persons we had harmed, and became willing to make amends to them all.

9. Made direct amends to such people wherever possible, except when to do so would injure them or others.

10. Continued to take personal inventory and when we were wrong promptly admitted it.

11. Sought through prayer and meditation to improve our conscious contact with God *as we understood Him*, praying only for knowledge of His will for us and the power to carry that out.

12. Having had a spiritual awakening as the result of these steps, we tried to carry this message to alcoholics, and to practice these principles in all our affairs.

The recovery groups that grew out of Alcoholics Anonymous, which run the gamut from Emotions Anonymous to Gang Anonymous, are now helping to combat a variety of addictions worldwide. Their grateful members are one-by-one discovering a Higher Power that is turning their personal defeats into victories.

After conversing with hundreds of people in recovery programs for substance abuse or destructive behavior, I decided to augment the available literature on recovery by providing spiritual commentary on the divinely inspired Twelve Steps, which is what this book attempts to do. It explores the Steps' implied yet rarely stated spiritual potential for clearing away the debris we have accumulated on the downward spiral of addiction and for guiding us back to ourselves and our Higher Power. Its guidance can serve as a valuable adjunct to any recovery program, or for anyone in need of a broader spiritual perspective to start their recovery.

Each segment of this book opens in the fashion of a meeting—with a testimony from a recovering addict, revealing their struggles on the road to freedom. Although some of these life stories are raw and at times shocking, they demonstrate the honesty and courage needed for full and sustained recovery. Here you will find firsthand accounts from people I have interviewed who are maintaining sobriety from cocaine, compulsive overeating, obsessive sex, habitual gambling, narcotics, overspending, alcohol, obsessive codependence, difficulties in living with an alcoholic, overworking, an addiction in conjunction with a diagnosed psychiatric disorder, and nicotine. For each, the height of their addiction was the depth of their pain.

Following the testimony is the Step it illuminates, which has been named to signify the personal trait that is required to master its lessons. To offer heart-to-heart assistance, each Step closes with a series of reflections that can be used in quiet moments to help you move inward or to link you directly to your Higher Power. These essays, which emerged from the promptings of my inner being, have transported innumerable people with diverse addictions into spiritual consciousness. In other words, they work.

The final chapter, "Continuing On in Recovery," presents simple practices to promote harmony and balance. Incorporating these disciplnes into your life as you continue walking the steps will move you toward ever deeper levels of self-honoring.

The appendixes at the back of the book contain practical resources to assist you on your journey. Here you will find self-tests—short "quizzes" to help you determine if you or a loved one may have crossed the line from a pleasurable pastime to a hard-core addiction due to one of the twelve compulsive behaviors referred to throughout these pages. Here, too, is contact information for the relevant Twelve-Step support groups. At the conclusion of the book is a listing of volumes with a proven track record for enhancing spiritual attunement.

Although *Honoring Your Self* was written for people in recovery programs, it offers guidance for *anyone* interested in self-growth or personal development. The deadening forces of addiction, after all, come in big and small packages: from alcoholism and drugs to a thousand little habits and routines that distance us from our feelings, other people, and above all, spirit.

However you define your personal challenges, delve freely into these pages to improve your quality of life and to honor the being in the center of your heart. Reach for a reflection any time you need comfort, fortification, or the courage to take a major step forward. May your journey bring you unthinkable treasures, and may you, as Ralph Waldo Emerson said in his *Journal,* feel it an honor to wash your face, being as it is, the temple of spirit.

Alicia

—A Member of Cocaine Anonymous—

I began using at about fourteen years old. I was terrified of everything, and the drugs and alcohol stopped me from being so scared. It got to a point, when I was about twenty-five, that there was nothing in my life but drugs and alcohol. I did the drugs and drank to come down. I used cocaine, acid, and crystal, but what really got to me was the crack; I used it for eight months. I'd cruise down the street wanting to drive into a wall, but because I was a mother—I have a son—I couldn't do that.

Instead, I made myself a wreck. I had a massage therapy business, and I decided if I didn't answer my pager I wouldn't have to work. Then I figured if I didn't have a car I wouldn't need to drive. So, I traded my $10,000 car for five rocks of crack. I didn't want anything else. I just wanted to get high.

The turning point came one night in a hotel room, where I was doing crack with a friend. I'd been to a couple of Twelve-Step meetings, and some things I heard there really hit home. Even though I never sat through a whole meeting, I had this feeling inside of me that I was done. So when my friend said, "Let's go get another rock," I went out to her car with her, stopped in my tracks, and told her, "I'm done." And it was like, *where did that come from?*

I walked back to my mother's house, and Mama reached out her arms and said, "Did you hit a bottom?" I just looked at her and said, "I don't know what I did, but I'm terrified." So I started going to meetings and staying till the end—sometimes three, sometimes four a day. Cocaine Anonymous, Alcoholics Anonymous, anything I could find.

Nine days later I went to a treatment center where peers help each other and people come to speak. One guy told us this story of "The Addict in the Hole":

There's an addict, and he's in a hole. A pit. And he's screaming for people to help him. A priest walks by, and the addict yells, "Help me! Help me get out of this hole." The priest throws him a rope, and the addict jumps and jumps but can't reach it. So then the priest shrugs his shoulders and walks off. Pretty soon, a doctor walks by, and the addict yells, "Help me! Help me get out of this hole." The doctor throws him a rope, and the addict tries to reach it but can't. The doctor pretty much shrugs his shoulders and keeps walking.

The man then screams at a recovering addict who happens to be walking by. And the recovering addict jumps in the hole with him. The first addict says, "What did you do that for? Now we're both stuck." And the second addict says, "I've been here, and I know the way out."

When I heard that, tears rolled down my face. I knew I'd finally found help and could beat my habit.

After the program at the center, I became a regular at Cocaine Anonymous, which has given me a relationship with God—a constancy in a life that had nothing. Either God is there or he isn't, and for me he is. In the middle of the night when I scream and cry and beg, he's there.

My mom died the day after I completed my fourteenth month in recovery. She got to see me sober, and to see the change God made in my life. Even though she wasn't a drug addict or anything, she wanted that kind of change herself. Then she's about to die, and the first thing I see is a shooting star. And I'm screaming, "A shooting star, and I'm on my way to the hospital to see my dying mother." I said, "Thy will be done." This was possible only because of the surrender that I had learned.

Surrender

*I hereby surrender all my addictions
so that I can face the morning sun
of myself without blinking.*

For Alicia and many others, addiction is a three-pronged disease: a physical compulsion, a mental obsession, and a spiritual starvation. As for me, although I didn't physically abuse myself with alcohol, I was mentally obsessed with drinking and experienced acute spiritual starvation. Such spiritual depletion is an extremely strong motivator; indeed, it is the bottom of the most precious bottle—the desperate emptiness that leads us to take that first brave step.

When I was fired from a good sales job because of my drinking, I considered it a first-class disaster. Right away, I sought out a prostitute despite a personal vow never to pay for sex. Although we ended up only talking, I had been driven to violate my moral code again. This was a good example of how drinking had eroded my sense of personal integrity. As I walked away from this encounter, I was disgusted with myself.

The next day I had reached the bottom and finally took the critical step of surrendering my addiction. I was sick and tired of being sick and tired: I woke up every morning with a hangover, my finances were a shambles, and I was riddled with guilt from lying to others and to myself. In short, my life had become unmanageable. And it was my birthday. I was staying in a hotel room and had turned on the radio to hear Tennessee Ernie Ford's rendition of "In the Garden." My desperate plight as an alcoholic, linked with this reminder of my childhood faith, brought me literally to my knees.

In admitting that I was powerless over alcohol, and in finally whispering, "Yes, I'm an alcoholic" to the bull's-eye question asked by my rehab counselor, Sister Ignatia, I had thrown in the towel. I felt great tears of relief as I gave up and surrendered to a truth I had denied for nearly five years. The act of surrendering set the stage for the next chapter of my life: my battle against addiction. At this ground-zero point, I also discovered the power of prayer. So it was that the disaster of being fired from my job became the catalyst to an exciting new existence—a life of sobriety.

Whatever our craving—alcohol, drugs, sex, gambling, overeating, overworking, or cigarettes—we eventually learn that even ironclad willpower is ineffective when the addiction takes control of us. This is when we recognize that we are "powerless." During the five-year period in which I tried to stop drinking, I discovered that the needed strength could come only from praying to a Higher Power. Sounds easy, doesn't it? Just pray like a little child and you will succeed, one day at a time. But although it may sound simple, it took a series of small disasters, a few big defeats, and much trying and failing before I sought out the spiritual connection that helped me succeed.

The worldwide popularity of the many Twelve-Step programs shows the success of these principles in helping people recover from various addictions. The First Step is the most important. Admitting that we are "powerless" over a substance or behavior that has been hanging like an albatross around our necks, is a breakthrough to be accompanied by celebration. For it is admission and then surrender that starts our recovery. For years I had carefully avoided taking this first big step, out of conceit and pride. I had told myself that I could beat any bloody thing, even alcohol, with willpower. Yet only when I stepped down from my pulpit, knelt on the hallowed ground of humility, and said, "I need help; I can't do it alone," did I begin the Twelve-Step journey to freedom.

The following four reflections delve into Step One's theme of how unmanageable our lives have become, how seemingly powerless we are in the grip of our addictions, and the healing power of surrender. As you read them in a quiet corner of your life—or better yet, in the midst of chaos—allow them to gently open your heart to the presence of your Higher Power. Reflection 1, "The Law of Opportunity," shows us that opportunity presents itself at particular moments and in different guises, inviting us, if we are ready, to advance to the next stage of our lives. Reflection 2, "Catnip," explores the dark world of addictions and cults, as well as the liberating path of disentanglement. Reflection 3, "Another View of Riotous Living," offers insight into why many addicts stumble down the trail of "wine, women, and song." Reflection 4, "Love and Hate," portrays these two emotions as flip sides of each other, and explains why addicts usually end up hating someone they love—often, themselves.

The Law of Opportunity

We all participate in one of God's great laws: the Law of Opportunity. There is a story about a young man, born into the British royal household and in line to become king, who was one day soundly lectured about his obligation to his English subjects. Shaking his head, he told his senior advisor, "I want to stay the way I am." Regrettably, many people are reluctant to increase their responsibility toward their fellow humans. Some fear that if they move beyond the status quo of their lives, they will be shattered by influences they cannot handle. In effect, they are unwilling to surrender to a higher force.

The Law of Opportunity reminds us that to seize a fresh chance to advance to the next grade in the School of Life, we must often leave behind our fellow students and teachers, and move on to a new classroom. However, such drastic change should be undertaken only when the student is prepared. First, we must master our current tasks, learning our lessons and passing our tests; then we may obey the gentle nudging of our angels, our own inner voices, to pick up our books and progress.

Often, we will not receive this new direction on cue. It may require a waiting period, time in which other matters should be addressed until the proper path is shown and the new course made clear. We must keep listening, however, because the direction may be revealed quite unexpectedly. For example, opportunity might be dressed in the garb of its twin sister, disaster. Rarely do we think there is promise lurking in situations that appear hopeless, such as a serious reversal of good fortune, or the loss of a job or material possessions; yet catastrophe is one of opportunity's favorite disguises. Plato put it this way: Inspiration comes like a light kindled from a leaping spark which, having reached the soul, finds its own fuel.

In the simple yet profound act of taking the First Step—acknowledging that our lives are unmanageable and then surrendering our addiction—we clear out the clutter and prepare for a cleaner, truer walk to the yonder foothills of spiritual peace. For when we allow the Law of Opportunity to manifest in our lives, we realize that we are not alone: in addition to support group members, we have a host of spiritual friends eager to help us recover our divine balance and smooth the path ahead.

Friendly advice is as likely to come from a stranger as from a loved one, or from a dream, a wish, or a sudden repugnance to our addiction. We can best respond by quietly withdrawing into ourselves and listening to the wisdom arising from within. When the way is made clear, we will know the proper course to take, allowing the Law of Opportunity to draw us closer to our ultimate goal.

Catnip

Catnip, made from certain aromatic leaves, has an unusual effect on felines. Once they smell or taste it, they become playful, carefree bundles of fur with no aim in life other than to frolic, roll languidly on the ground, and continue to smell the magical substance before them. Humans have their own "catnip response" to a variety of stimuli in their physical and mental worlds, some of the most potent of which come in the form of opiates. These drugs can render their users sleepy and inoperative, subject only to their personal whims and desires, and focused solely on their own thoughts and fantasies.

Users isolate themselves from mainstream activities, dwelling in eddies or pools apart from the river of human consciousness. There they undergo no mental or spiritual growth, but only a languid, rolling-on-the-floor existence in which the catnip becomes the only reality. The difference between catnip fantasies and real living on "manna from heaven" is akin to the classic distinction between forces of darkness and light. Whatever the agent—alcohol, drugs, food, sex, gambling, work—addiction's great curse is that it plunges the person into a form of solitary confinement, into their own narrow world of perception that prevents them from contributing to the greater world of spirit we all share.

Worse, an addict's imagination runs rampant, building castles of hope, escapism, and retreat within purely subjective realms. If mind is the builder, as Edgar Cayce would say, imagination is the architect. When used constructively, imagination designs realms where people share, connect, and rejoice together in sacred communion. Used negatively, however, this precious creative power can summon up hellish domains that further distance us from our divine source and inspiration. Under the guise of exploration, some addicts delve into satanic cults and rituals—a catnip response that leaves them debilitated, their energies sapped for useful service, and their lives diverted from spiritual truth and peace.

Addictions tend to trigger escapades of this sort—detours around the beautiful "classroom" God has created for us to enjoy, to learn from, and to pass on in an improved state to the next generation. Yet catnip begins to loosen its powerful grip on us as we gather with like-minded people, or as we talk or pray together. A vigilant awareness of a Higher Power can guide us back from this strange terrain to our true home. Neither mind nor willpower alone will steer us free of self-destruction; only surrender to the force we call God or our Higher Power can redirect our energies toward a constructive, addiction-free future. We must engage in earnest prayer, raising our hearts to spirit like children untainted by cynicism, doubt, or fear of the world.

For solace, we need only remember that people throughout the world remain dedicated to illuminating the spiritual path so that others may follow it. Churches of all faiths offer weary travelers a chance to rekindle their energies and redirect their courses. Spiritual leaders such as Billy Graham, Rabbi Zalman Schachter-Shalomi, the Dalai Lama, and Sai Baba guide millions in quickening their spiritual pulse, thereby helping us to help ourselves.

"Let the lower lights be burning. Send the gleam across the waves. Some poor struggling, starving seaman you may rescue, you may save." These words from an old hymn remind us of our ability to rescue ourselves by keeping a watchful eye out for the light upon the shore—for the Higher Power that forever conquers darkness.

REFLECTION 3

Another View of Riotous Living

Riotous living is a life of debauchery, loose or easy morals, unbridled passions—or, as the Big Book of Alcoholics Anonymous describes it, "self-will run riot." A will engaged in such indulgences is using outer sensations to try to reverse a state of spiritual starvation. Once-virtuous people who have slipped into spiritual malaise will often depart from their prosaic paths and take up riotous living, with purple passion and song and dance holding sway for several years. Others will have a "fling," leading to many of the same consequences.

Driven by self-will and a fear of surrender, subscribers to riotous living soon become tempest-tossed on seas of lust and dissipation—their God, transformed into a distant blinking star, partially eclipsed by the prevailing forces of darkness; their bodies, wretched gathering places for all manner of diseases; their minds, perplexed and disoriented. Instead of laughter and joy and real communion, these people are aware only of the pain and loneliness of a life lived apart from a Higher Power's love and guidance.

Former addicts know how necessary it is to hit bottom before redirecting their course from debauchery to serenity. After the detour is over and they have managed to push aside the lower self and let a Higher Power pour through them, they go on to lead beautiful lives of surrender to God's will for them. With the lessons they have learned etched deeply in their memories, they carry a fresh resolve to seek spirit, come what may, in every aspect of their lives. This rebound from riotous living frequently awakens not only a desire to live in the realm of spirit but also the *energy* to do so. Great heights can be scaled by those who have sunk to the depths.

In fact, many pious people in our communities, both past and present, have rebounded from the painful experience of riotous living. Captain John Newton, a slave trader who penned the song "Amazing Grace" ("I once was lost, but now am found"), was undoubtedly once the wretch he described. So, too, were numerous present-day champions who are now beckoning us to take the path of spirit. Because they have lived life fully, their call is inspiring and their words bear the stamp of authenticity.

This long view broadens our perspective on individuals who, having embraced perversity and self-will, now lie beached on the shoals of self-destruction. We need only remember that when high tide returns, as surely it will, the ship will sail free, and its course will run true to the single great star that illuminates all heavens and all hearts.

If you are now temporarily submersed in the sands of riotous living, peace to you. May you learn your lessons well, and return to spirit with great love and rejoicing.

REFLECTION 4

Love and Hate

Human beings have long beheld an object of desire with the contrary emotions of love and hate. Why, they have wondered, should such opposing forces be directed at the same person? Why can't we feel either one emotion or the other?

It seems that the forces of love and hate replenish each other. The situation might be compared to a reciprocating engine, in which one piston thrusts against the drive shaft while another pauses for a gulp of fuel before exchanging functions with its resting companion. In other words, it could be that, since human emotions expend energy, a steady stream of fuel is needed to maintain a desired feeling such as love.

Furnishing an inexhaustible stream of love takes constant subconscious effort, some of which must be intermittently supplied by its opposite, hatred. At such times the beloved, as if viewed through dense clouds, is beheld as an object to be despised, rejected, and castigated. In fact, the more powerful the love is, the more intense the hatred is apt to be—much to the consternation of the lover, who cannot account for such an upsurge of negativity.

What is not apparent to those who love each other, or to those who have great affinity for an art form or a religious or political ideology, is that a switch in polarity provides a rejuvenating force, permitting ongoing love for the cherished person, or renewed dedication to the revered work of art or ideology. In other words the polarity, a natural component of human nature, is necessary for maintaining a steady supply of pure energy. If this dynamic were more widely understood, we would be less likely to "push the panic button" every time a contrary emotion overtakes us. We would learn to surrender to the flow—the yin and yang, as Taoists call it—of God's laws at work in the human heart. It might also reduce the growing number of suicides by those who walk on the shadow side of the street unaware that the sunny side is only yards to the north.

Certainly, a better understanding of the love-hate dynamic would revitalize the sacred institution of marriage. Currently, the contrary energies aroused by these twin emotions are escalating the divorce rate rather than recharging the spiritual batteries of partners. Viewed through the lens of polarity, however, they can help us see beyond the shadows cast by the clouds, and teach us to wait patiently for the reemergence of love's light to help us continue attending to our heart's desires.

Sally

I'm a compulsive overeater. I can't remember a time when food wasn't at the hub of my existence. At birthday parties and during Christmas, I never cared about presents or people—only food. I can even tell you the color of my birthday cake when I turned three.

When I was a preteen, my mother became chief of the Food Police. (By the way, I had wonderful parents, so I can't blame *them* for my overeating.) Then at age thirteen, I had my first experience with a diet doctor and amphetamines. All they did was make me a fast eater. I dieted at home and ate on the outside. I had a horrendous high school career; I never dated or anything—never even hoped to—although I did have some girlfriends.

Between high school and college, I lost a lot of weight, so my college years were actually pretty good. But soon my food addiction reared its ugly head and I was on a perpetual round of dieting-eating, dieting-eating. It consumed my life.

Soon after college, I married a wonderful man and birthed three babies in two and a half years. I kept some weight on after each one, and again my life revolved around dieting and eating. When I wasn't thinking about changing diapers, I was fixated on food—either staying away from it or gorging on it. Nothing else mattered, just my kids and food.

When I was thirty-one years old, my husband died suddenly of a heart attack. Bundling up our three young children, I moved us from California to the Southwest, thinking that relocating would help me lose weight, which of course it didn't. After six weeks in the Southwest, I married someone who turned out to be a sociopath. He rapidly depleted all my resources and demoralized me. I had one child with him, then adopted his daughter. Five years later I divorced him, which left me fat, sad, broke … and a single mom of five kids.

In California I somehow got my life in order and applied to graduate school. Feeling pretty good, I gave myself permission to eat. But within six months, I had gained 45 pounds—weighing in at 215—was in the throes of sugar blackouts, and felt really desperate. It was unbelievable the quantities of food I would ingest!

Then in connection with one of my courses, I attended a workshop called Alcohol and the Older Adult. It was presented by an AA counselor, who started off by giving us a test about drinking. Since alcohol had never been a problem in my life, thank God, all my answers were "no." But suddenly—I'm sure it was my first spiritual experience—God had me replace "alcohol" and "drinking" with "food" and "eating." Out of the fifteen questions, I now had twelve yesses. I came away thinking something was wrong with me, something far more serious than a lack of willpower or poor moral standards.

The very next night, I went to my first Overeaters Anonymous meeting, and by the grace of God I got it! I mean, I was struck abstinent at the meeting. And thanks to the people in the fellowship, I have maintained that abstinence pretty cleanly. I won't say *perfectly*, but it has been a strong abstinence. I now weigh 140 pounds, I work out, and I'm pretty healthy. Best of all, I have a God box. Any time something bothers me, I write it down and stuff it in the box. Then I feel hopeful, because I know the problem's in much better hands than mine.

Hope

*I'm beginning to believe I can receive help
from an unexpected source, and that if I accept it
this help will undoubtedly change my life.*

When I knelt down to pray in the hotel room on my forty-second birthday, I wasn't convinced that a power greater than myself could help me. Instead, I took it on faith—on what remained of my childhood faith in God. Although raised by a devout father and an idealistic mother, I had abandoned this faith. Looking for someone to talk with as an adult, I frequented bars, desperately seeking help in all the wrong places. Then there in the hotel room, the hymn "In the Garden" filled me with an old, familiar feeling of hope. So it was that in surrendering my self-will to God, I was returning home, like the prodigal son.

Every living being seems to have a spiritual instinct that sends it on a return journey at one time or another. No tour guide tells salmon where to lay their eggs. Similarly, no booming voice from the heavens said, "Hob, get down on your knees if you want to climb out of this mess." Hope doesn't present itself that way. Instead, after we send out a sincere plea for help, a surge of promise usually rises up through the subtle texture of our lives, sparked by an unexpected phone call from an old friend, or a casual comment from a coworker. In my case, I just "happened" to turn on the radio to Tennessee Ernie Ford's rendition of one of my favorite childhood tunes.

While catapulting us to safety, this spiritual impulse also draws to us the helping hand we so desperately need. For me the need was urgent. Feeling moderately insane, I required immediate assistance from someone, anyone—so much so that the old hymn melted my heart, lowered me to my knees, and tuned me in to the silence of my own heart for guidance. It was there I hoped to find the sanity my addiction had been smothering.

An essential aspect of Step Two is knowing the difference between trying to live life on one's own terms and allowing God to provide constant support. Reflection 5, "Going it Alone?" explores how difficult the path of self-will can be. Reflection 6, "Staying Connected in Times of Great Change," addresses this era of tumultuous change and our Higher Power's capacity to carry us through the chaos. Reflection 7, "The Magic Ingredients of Hope and Faith," shows how hope and faith can help us fulfill our greatest wishes. Reflection 8, "Shall We Dance?" examines the violence and unpredictability of the natural world, and urges us to seek the constancy of spirit.

Going It Alone?

Being overly self-reliant, self-governing, and self-ruling leads to isolation, for it disrupts our communion with all that is. Heeding self as the supreme authority also exposes us to great danger in a world with many pitfalls. For example, after succeeding in a business venture, we may conclude that God's grace or our soul's karma did not contribute to the accomplishment but rather we alone were responsible for it. Such an attitude can bloat the ego and subject us to forces beyond our control. Or greed for money, power, or authority may seduce us into overestimating our capacities and, as a result, committing fatal errors of judgment. In both instances, fears arise—inner demons that shackle the mind, cloud our vision, and paralyze us with tension. Addicts and nonaddicts alike, stalked by these forbidding terrors, have been driven further and further into isolation.

Rather than floundering in trial and error, how much wiser we would be to move forward under spiritual direction. Tremendous productivity is available in partnering with a Higher Power, each day acknowledging its sacred inner presence and welcoming its loving guidance. Further, the greatest comfort and companionship come from entrusting our lives and care to such a power, and from feeling so completely accepted by it. Once established in this partnership, we can look back to when an addictive substance controlled us, and there we would discover long periods when a divine presence was imperceptible to us. Like a blind person in a crowd, we groped for help yet invariably reached out to the wrong people for support.

Although many addicts have lost sight of it, our most precious possession is this awareness of the Higher Power's presence in our lives, and of our existence as both children of God and one with God. No longer must we stumble and fall, or feel compelled to strike out at others. No longer must we be alone in our despair. Instead, glowing with the fire of divine awareness, we can set forth each day with mighty confidence and strength.

St. Augustine waited many years before recognizing God. When forced into a dark corner, he finally cried out for guidance, only to learn that his Higher Power had been there all along. So, too, can each of us awaken to this awareness, for we are wrapped in sleep and forgetfulness. First, however, we must make an effort to connect with spirit by grasping its outstretched hand, allowing its fingers to cradle us ever so gently.

How do we recognize our Higher Power? This is a mystery each of us must solve for ourselves. When the apostle Paul, on the road to Damascus to kill more Christians, was struck dumb and blind by a bright light, there was no question of God's intervention. Most of us are not so fortunate. We addicts are more like watchmen on the turrets of a castle, waiting to see the first faint rays of morning—a sign that the darkness is finally abating.

When we have connected with our Higher Power, how do we lead others to recognize *their* spiritual selves? The worst way is through self-righteous preaching. The best is by example: by holding meetings with other addicts in a clean spiritual atmosphere, allowing each person's emerging self to breathe in the unpolluted air of our freedom, to experience a life lived close to spirit. The key is in knowing at every moment where we came from and where we are going.

Staying Connected in Times of Great Change

This is a restless juncture in history. Many people are questioning their self-worth and wanting to accelerate their growth. In response, they are seeking opportunities to dramatically alter their lives, going off on exotic trips to faraway lands, buying expensive homes and vehicles, cultivating an atmosphere of constant excitement. It is the nature of the times; the vast ocean of humanity seems to be seething and roiling beneath its sometimes placid surface.

It is said that the average Westerner experiences more in one day than our ancestors of only 500 years ago experienced in a lifetime. Why has the pace of life speeded up so drastically and the diversity of human exposures expanded so broadly? According to some, an upsurge of spirit is moving through our lives. And with each heave has come an amplified connection to everything around us, enabling us to attain new heights of awareness, deeper communion with all life forms, and increased understanding of our essential oneness with the universe. Spiritual values are rising to the fore—a human potential that has lain dormant for thousands of years.

In the last seventy-five years, the average human being has gone from traveling by train between cities to taking supersonic jets across continents, from conversing by telephone to communicating over the Internet, from tapping out messages on Underwood typewriters to using personal computers with hard drives equipped to store more information than a library of books. With such major changes occurring so rapidly, it is no wonder many of us reel about like blind sailors attempting to steer their ships through a raging storm.

Fortunately, because of our expanded awareness, we are better able to hear the quiet voice of the Higher Power that guides us, keeps us on course, and helps us in times of turbulence, saying, as the psalmist David wrote, "Be still, and know that I am God." So it is that with risk comes opportunity—in this case, the chance to know that our protector is indeed here to navigate us through the squalls and keep us pointed toward our home port.

REFLECTION 7

The Magic Ingredients of Hope and Faith

*H*ope that what we desire is obtainable, combined with *faith* in our Higher Power, are the growth ingredients par excellence. They can be compared to the yeast a baker adds to dough while making bread or pastry. Yeast's fermenting properties transforms ordinary flour and water into something edible and nourishing. Without this magical leaven, the wet dough would remain inert.

Hope and faith are the twin energies of transformation. Hope is what stirs within individuals who yearn for the city to be built, the child to grow to adulthood, the field to flourish come harvesttime. Faith, on the other hand, calls upon a godlike creative spark within to transform dreams into reality. It is through this perception of ourselves as spiritual beings that our desires become manifest *when and if they are in keeping with our Higher Power's plan for us.*

Hope keeps the universe moving on schedule. It fertilizes the seed that later yields a plentiful crop. It propels the toss of the angler's net cast out toward a school of fish. It is the all-important flare that ignites the scholar searching for truth in a dusty book, or in the complexities of human behavior. Hope is the thrust that carries scientists into the sky to unravel cosmic mysteries, or into microscopic realms to uncover the natural laws of microbes and atoms—all for the benefit of humanity.

Faith gives birth to new miracles. Many people who pray for divine assistance begin with an act of faith, in which they thank God in advance for all that is about to transpire. History is filled with such acts of faith performed by Jesus, Muhammad, Moses, and David, as well as other prophets and spiritual masters. When we have hope that our prayers will be answered, and have faith in our Higher Power to manifest them, mighty results cannot help but follow.

The dual forces of hope and faith also help us transform our *personal* lives. Through the daily repetition of simple prayers, an endeavor that attunes us to these forces, we can remember our true roles and overcome our inertia. Constant practice is as necessary for self-transformation as it is for transforming a lump of dough or a barren field. And so we practice prayer, and in the process we learn that we do indeed control our destiny—that God helps those who help themselves—at which point we can turn to the divine fire of faith to light our way.

REFLECTION 8

Shall We Dance?

Shall we dance in celebration of spring or gaze back at winter, shaking a fist at its ice-cold frigidity? Let us welcome *each* season's joys and inclemencies as opportunities to experience Mother Nature's handiwork—the cloth that spirit weaves around us.

A rugged winter, a summer heat wave, hurricanes, blizzards, tornadoes, tidal waves, floods, and earthquakes all increase our awareness of spirit's presence. We see in them a force beyond our control that shakes the very foundations of our hand-built shelters and routs birds' nests, burns wild animals' food caches, pollutes earth's waters. This power is much greater than our own, which is flickering, candlelike, in the darkness.

The destruction in nature shows us that God's universe keeps changing—that what is created in one form is soon transmuted into another, and yet another. Only its creator remains immutable. The good news is that in aligning ourselves with this unchanging essence of spirit, through a relationship with our Higher Power, we become fortified to withstand the changes in the natural world, and in our tumultuous private worlds as well.

When winds howl from the north, or rivers rise, or the sun scorches the fields, let us be aware of God's control over all that is. And when the stars reappear following the winds' last sigh, let us offer our deepest gratitude to our Higher Power, which guides us until the end of our lives, and far, far beyond.

Joshua

—A Member of Sex and Love Addicts Anonymous—

I used to be a prosecuting attorney, and sex was my first drug of choice. I came from a physically abusive background. Brutalized by my mother—bound, gagged, and beaten—I started to dissociate early on, going off into my own world. By the time I was twelve, masturbation had become a way of release. Then I began voyeurism with masturbation, because it was a way of exciting myself further, like using cocaine with alcohol.

As soon as I started dating, I was involved in multiple relationships. Living on a farm near several towns allowed me to have girlfriends in each one, none of whom knew about the others. It was a pattern I continued throughout my adult life. However, my most recent relationship before coming into Sex and Love Addicts Anonymous (SLAA) was different. This partner was dogged about tracking down the other women in my life. By then, I was living in a small town, and any time she heard that I was even talking to another woman, she would seek her out and virtually run her off. It was very embarrassing.

So I decided to change my ways, to have just one relationship … And lo and behold, the voyeurism showed up again. I was caught, tried, and prosecuted. Suspended by the Bar Association, I also lost my career. The story was in the newspapers, as well as on radio and TV. It was a public shaming of unbelievable magnitude.

I went to The Meadows, a facility directed by Patrick Carnes, author of *Out of the Shadows*, which I knew was a book about sexual addictions. Everyone at my first SLAA meeting had been talking about it; so I read the book, but it didn't apply. After this last situation, though, I realized how much it *did* apply, and I used it throughout my recovery.

Now I no longer have multiple relationships. My bottom-line behavior is, I am not doing sex—a decision that has caused me to go through significant pain, withdrawal, and reflections on my childhood. I've tried to see who I am and why I'm where I'm at, and how my addictive behaviors were destroying my life.

The Twelve-Step SLAA program gives me a haven, a place to go. It's better for me than AA, because there you can't talk about sexual relationships very easily. If you stand up at an AA meeting and say, "I'm a sex addict and I like to window peek and masturbate," or "I fondle little girls," or "I like little boys," you're going to trigger a real negative reaction. But at SLAA I can talk about my sexual drives, my compulsions, my love addictions—it's all acceptable. Sex and love obsessions are as unrecognized now as alcoholism was in the 1940s, before the medical community decided it was an addictive behavior.

I have no doubt that sex is an addiction. Although I often used alcohol as a subterfuge, when I said I was sorry my regrets had more to do with my sexual acting out, having multiple relationships, as well as sleeping around on people and getting caught. The crippling emotion of shame is what keeps this addiction such a secret, and secrets keep people sick. But if you can let the secret out of the bag and stop the destructive behaviors, you start to feel different. The mortifying shame finally gives way to a new life through the promise of faith.

Faith

*When I have faith, I will discover inner resources strong
enough to allow me to walk over hot coals without blistering.
If others with the same addiction are making that walk,
then so can I.*

How do we arrive at the point of willingly turning our lives over to God's care? For some addicts, this change of heart takes a major shake-up—incarceration, a job dismissal, or a child's disappointment. Until that time, our every move feels as though we are shoveling sand against a rising tide. The more we resist God's will, the deeper the hole we dig with each small fix or stopgap measure, until finally we see that our surrender must be complete—that we must reach out with total faith.

To make this leap of faith, we must first know what we are entrusting our lives *to*. We each have our own definition of God, informed by our childhood experiences, cultural and religious background, and life exposures. In fact, how a person perceives God is as unique as their fingerprints. What matters is not the special name we give this Supreme Being, but rather why its presence feels so loving and nurturing. With that, we can have faith in its beneficence.

Deciding to turn our lives over to God's care may inspire us to attend Twelve-Step meetings. There some people start by simply observing others, researching the issues, and getting a feel for the territory. It can take a while to feel comfortable with the proceedings. Then, when the quiet voice within announces that the time is right, active participation begins. When we actively participate in these meetings, we are entrusting ourselves to God's care.

Human beings are, at heart, very wise and knowledgeable. To reconnect with this divine wisdom, however, we must first strip away such notions as "I make my own rules," "I am the invincible master of my fate," and "I'm going to do it all myself." For me, the illusion of self-sufficiency began to dissolve when I recognized that I could not stop drinking on my own. Only then did I realize I could not manage without God's assistance.

Step Three helps us develop both an inner understanding of our Higher Power and trust in its capacity to improve the way we lead our lives. Reflection 9, "How to Find Truth," describes why truth is hidden and how best to find it. Reflection 10, "Beauty Springs from Awareness," explains how spiritual development leads to a more refined appreciation of beauty. Reflection 11, "The Struggle for Perfection," illustrates the importance of overcoming obstacles. Reflection 12, "'Do' versus 'Be Done,'" portrays the difference between actively doing God's will and passively allowing God's will to be done.

REFLECTION 9

How to Find Truth

When we entrust ourselves to the care of our Higher Power, we begin a journey that opens us to all that is true in the world. Instead of waking up each morning with another hangover, downer, or bout of remorse, we open our eyes to God's precious gift of truth. But why, you may ask, is this treasure so elusive?

Truth is the one constant in an ever-changing world where God's spirit animates all things. When God set in motion the forces that created our universe, certain physical and spiritual laws were established that now guide all of creation. These laws can be seen in the uniformity and exactitude of a carpenter's measurements, even in the 90-degree angle at which a mason lays a cornerstone. From these laws come the towering skyscrapers of the modern world.

Truth, then, is the animating force at the point of an inception; it is the first step of a journey, the first stone laid for an edifice, the first breath of a new creation. Yet it lies hidden from view—obscured by prejudice, vanity, and the chimera of self-sufficiency. As such, the quest for truth is for many people a lifelong pursuit.

How does one find these underlying laws of creation? As it is said in the Bible, "Seek and ye shall find; knock and the door shall be opened unto you." But seek for the right reason, keeping the Golden Rule in mind; and have faith that the door will be opened. Also, remember to proceed at God's pace, not yours—for if you storm the gates of creation, they may only clang shut before you. Let precipitous action and hurried activity yield to patience. Then you will find the oyster, and its shell will open to reveal its pearl of wisdom.

Some revelations of truth appear in a flash; others drift out to us a piece at a time. All revelations require self-discovery, for no one else can give us an understanding of truth. Once it is discovered, truth evokes unmistakable delight—a sign that we have found the elusive treasure. Such delight is often described in biblical parables, for example. The leper jumped for joy when Jesus cured him of his sickness (fallacy) and presented him with the gift of perfect health (truth). The blind man could hardly believe his good fortune when, after years of obscured vision (fallacy), he was given sight (truth).

REFLECTION 10

Beauty Springs from Awareness

Finding beauty in God's world, and an accompanying reverence for all creation, is another precious gift that comes with faith. We earn this bounty by staying with our recovery like plants cling to their roots.

Why, as we evolve spiritually, do we deepen our appreciation for beauty? Because our physical senses grow more acute, heightening our sensitivity to everything from subtle hues of light to musical vibrations, or the taste of honey, or the smell of freshly baked bread. It is as if we have been seeing only the eight colors of the rainbow, then discover that each one has sixty-four shades, and each shade has numerous hues. Similarly, over years of practicing visualization exercises, Buddhist meditators begin to see radiantly colorful deities with increasing vividness.

Although enhanced aesthetic appreciation is an outgrowth of every addict's spiritual development, no two of us are touched in quite the same way. The reason is that the degree to which we are moved by an aesthetic experience relates directly to the aptitudes and faculties we have developed in response to our particular life experiences. When it comes to music, for instance, acquired taste clearly governs a person's response. A native of Brazil's Amazon Jungle will react differently to a drumbeat than will his brother in the urban jungle of Sao Paulo; to farmhands in Missouri a violin concerto will sound nothing like it will to patrons of a concert hall in New York or Vienna.

Interestingly, the more sensitive we become to beauty in the world around us, the more apt we are to respond to the plight of our fellow humans. Having suffered through the torments of addiction, we will resonate more deeply with the strained faces of impoverished children and of rejected elders. Their unique beauty, striking chords within us, will move us deeply, for what we will be seeing in brief flashes is the spirit that dwells in us all.

Although the pull of spirit is much stronger than the tug of the full moon on earth's waters, some who see its flashes respond readily whereas others turn away. The differing reactions depend on one's relative awareness of God, suggesting that we humans see only what we have become.

Increased awareness of the beauty in God's creation is the alpha and omega of existence. It is said that such beauty is in the eye of the beholder. Actually, it is in their heart and soul.

The Struggle for Perfection

Athletes in training for an Olympic track meet must prepare to make personal sacrifices in order to break a record or win a gold medal. Hours of practice lead up to the final day of jumping higher, running faster, or flawlessly completing the triple axle. To make the mark, contestants must steadily improve their performance—an apt metaphor for addicts facing life's ongoing challenges. Although we might long for everlasting peace and tranquillity, we must prepare for the bitter disappointments, frustrations, and despair that characterize the ups and downs of an addiction-free existence.

Imagine a landscaped area in which the gardener has placed huge boulders to create rises and depressions, dividing what was previously level ground. The net effect may be a beautiful symmetry evoked by the contrasting terrain of a more natural setting. So it is with our inner landscapes: an overall effect of beauty will, in this case, depend on the manner in which we surmount the obstacles. So, don't despair when peace and tranquillity seem to elude you, for the forces of contention will bring a seed of promise. Water it, nurture it, and eat of its fruit as you consolidate your energy and prepare for the next thrust against your will and faith.

The step-by-step task of aligning with the perfection of our eternal nature is never completed. Yet, there is no other way to proceed. We reclaim spirit not by simply desiring its return but by struggling to perfect ourselves, and by expressing our love and devotion, our purity of thought and action, selflessness, and gratitude for our Higher Power's guidance. The road to heaven is paved with golden opportunities for service to humankind, and therefore to the Great Spirit.

When life is going badly, it can be difficult to understand that our ill fortune is the direct result of personal choice, as is our good fortune on better days. We volunteered to come to earth in order to restore our nature to its original perfection, as children of God. This "volunteer system" was devised by God to prompt us to grow, learn, and know.

So, while traversing the terrain of life, it is vital to keep sight of our overall course and our destination. The journey then becomes an impeccable combination of personal effort and divine guidance toward the ultimate goal we all seek.

REFLECTION 12

"Do" versus "Be Done"

There is a fine distinction between "doing God's will" and praying that "God's will be done." In doing God's will, we mobilize and direct our resources for purposes of following spiritual guidance. We commit every breath, every act to fulfilling God's will for us. Each day begins and ends with gratitude for the direction given and with energy for executing it faithfully. In our devotion we connect with others throughout the world who are dedicated to doing God's will and are infused with love, wisdom, and purpose. This is the highest goal we can achieve, the most rewarding task we can accomplish.

By contrast, when we pray that "thy will be done," we passively accept the omnipotence of God's will and become spectators at life's grand rugby match. Certainly, this is a pious desire that implies a degree of surrender; however, it lacks *commitment*. We are here, it seems, not to observe, but to actively align our free will, as well as all our personal resources, with God's will. In other words, our mission is not self-denial, but rather ever deeper levels of self-fulfillment.

With this in mind, it seems Jesus' counsel to pray is often misinterpreted to turn out passive religious subjects. Surely, Jesus was proposing that we pray for guidance, not supplant our free will and choice. Hence, those who wish to serve must come down from the bleachers and join the action on the playing field. Only by rubbing shoulders with friends and neighbors can we share the spirit moving through us, and thereby contribute to the well-being of one another.

"Faith without works is dead," the apostle James wrote. And indeed, great works come from rolling up our sleeves and engaging actively in the world. People who pray to God but feel no social obligation to humanity—who honor the *form* but not the *intent* of religious observance—contribute little to our world. They stand in stark contrast to sincere aspirants who quietly follow spirit through service to others.

We often delude ourselves into thinking we are praying faithfully while saying, "Thy will be done." To avoid falling into passivity, we might follow up with the key question: Done by *whom?* Better yet, let us pray for knowledge of God's will and then do everything in our power to act on it.

Tom

—A Member of Gamblers Anonymous—

I was into gambling for about two and a half years, and it was as if I'd been doing it all my life. It totally consumed me. It all started when casinos began popping up in my sales territory. I'd arrive at 8:00 in the morning, go to a machine, and by 4:30 in the afternoon I was rushing home to lie to my wife. Soon I had to make up really big lies because we no longer had a bank account.

The lack of self-worth is the issue I had to face squarely once I got into recovery. What steered me in this direction were several unconscious slips that alerted my wife to my gambling. I seemed to have set things up so that she would discover it. On some level I wanted to be caught; and when I was, the alternatives were not very pleasant. To avoid losing the light of my life—my soul mate—I went into a hospital addiction recovery program.

The hospital program was geared to all sorts of addictions, and out of fifteen people I was the only gambler. "What am I doing here?" I asked myself. "I'm so different from the rest of them. I'm not into alcohol or drugs." After four weeks, I realized that one addiction is like any other. Even so, when they said, "You've got to get to Gamblers Anonymous," I gave GA a try. Before long, I was sure I had the answers and didn't need meetings, and I actually did go for six months without gambling. I then decided I could take twenty bucks and gamble without a problem, going back only when I wanted. I did, and it worked out okay. Three weeks later was when the problem started. And it hit ten times harder than before. It snowballed—big time!

Once again I subconsciously set myself up for getting caught. By now, my wife was keeping the checkbook, and had it hidden in the trunk of her car. I took the second set of keys, unlocked the trunk, wrote a check for $200, and left the keys dangling from the keyhole—something I'd never done before. Later, as she was driving down the street, somebody stopped her and said, "Lady, you've got keys hanging from your trunk." She called me on the mobile phone and asked if I had anything to tell her. Realizing it was either do or die, I answered, "Yeah, and here's what's going on." I told her everything. She said, "I will go with you to the first GA meeting. Then it's up to you to continue if you want this relationship to last. It's your choice."

I've been going ever since. I've had lots of "using" dreams, gambling dreams, and one severe attack after about four weeks of sobriety. It was so strong that I was on my knees praying to God to take the desire away from me because I couldn't do it myself. That was the turning point. That was when I knew I could live in integrity and kick this habit if I walked hand in hand with God.

Integrity

*I hereby resolve to be
as honest with myself as possible.*

In Step Four, we ask ourselves what we have actually accomplished in our lives. (It is a Step to be tackled slowly and gently to avoid going into shock.) After we have taken an honest inventory, most of our excuses and justifications stand revealed, which can be a sobering experience. Whereas this self-assessment may hurl us back into denial, if we are serious about recovering we will eventually concede to reality and move into a state of integrity. Accepting ourselves, with all our flaws, helps us reclaim the self-confidence that addiction has destroyed. It also assists us in dealing with others, since we no longer need to lie about our shortcomings or exaggerate our self-importance.

Although taking a personal inventory is the Fourth Step in a Twelve-Step program, it is actually a procedure that recovering addicts perform all the time—while going to or coming from a meeting, as we lie in bed at night, and while in the shower. What is most important is the *honesty* we bring to the effort, and with it, the newfound ability to balance negatives with positives, which is easier now that we have tasted sobriety. For example, while working with integrity I discovered that if I did not look too long and hard in the mirror, I could see my true self more clearly and even begin to like what I saw.

Despite the budding awareness of our own goodness, holding on to anger, frustration, and resentment can trigger a return to our addiction.

One way to release grudges and resolve old anger is to list our resentments and talk about them with people we trust. My wife, for example, once gave me a card inscribed with the words "I now release all resentments and gratefully accept an overflowing abundance from our Father." I found this message so helpful that I kept it fastened to the lampshade in our bedroom, where it remains to this day.

Releasing resentments can be difficult, especially for those of us who are emotionally volatile. During my sales career, I was once cheated out of income, which made me hot with fury, so I reached for a bottle to douse the fire; fortunately, my reach exceeded my grasp. Now to guard against overreacting, I try to stand back and assess each unsettling circumstance. To protect my precious sobriety, I know I must keep an even keel and not get blown off center by every potentially threatening situation that arises.

So it is that Step Four has us take an objective, discerning, and thorough look at ourselves. In Reflection 13, "The Virtuous Life," we see that our faults each serve a purpose in our spiritual evolution. Reflection 14, "Better Ways of Learning," describes how our difficulties can teach us. Reflection 15, "The Middle Path," addresses the lessons we are here to learn as we progress from this lifetime to the next.

REFLECTION 13

The Virtuous Life

Virtuous human beings tend to hold their character defects safely in check. While dealing with other people, they strive to maintain the ideals of honesty, purity, unselfishness, and love. Adherence to these four ideals, all taught by the world's great religions, can elevate the consciousness of anyone fighting an addiction, and can help us gain moral ground.

All the while we may wonder, will I ever change enough to enjoy the freedom that comes from honoring my better self? In such times of doubt, we must remember two points: that each of us treads a unique path filled with learning experiences critical to our development, and that in the larger picture, acts lacking integrity help us confront our deficiencies. Pressing on, we can eventually redeem ourselves and experience a new phase of personal growth.

Sometimes addicts' learning experiences come roughly packaged; certainly, we appear to have an inordinate number of life-threatening wake-up calls. One person may have an accident or a debilitating illness that startles them into a spiritual response. Another, while serving a jail sentence, may for the first time hear the still, small voice of God. Such experiences, harsh as they may seem, can successfully jolt us out of our ingrained habits and routines.

For example, my twenty-five days in the Honolulu prison, especially the three spent in solitary confinement, were grueling. Yet later the experience reminded me that misguided actions could strip me of my freedom. I could see that if I drank again I would lose my precious freedom of thought and moral action.

As we pilgrims trudge toward our goals, it is well worth cultivating the virtue of honesty. It may take many unpleasant experiences with dishonesty before we can win such a prize; but having paid so dearly for it, we will weave it fully into the fabric of our immortal being. Aware of the gifts of sadness, the Sufi poet Rumi wrote, "How can I sell sorrow when you know it's a blessing?"

Likewise, the virtues of purity, unselfishness, and love may emerge only after much refinement. In this sense, cultivating virtue is much like smelting gold or any other fine metal: you apply intense heat, melt the mass, and let it cool, whereupon the metal loses its dross and manifests the purity of its true nature. Similarly, over the course of becoming virtuous, we must enter the fire of experience and burn off our impurities until our true self shines through. Attributes indigenous to the soul, such as dedication, help carry us through this often infernal process.

You need not fear the many twists and turns on the road to a virtuous life, for your Higher Power will be providing inspirational guideposts along the way: the counsel of fellow pilgrims, the bibles of world religions, psychotherapy, Twelve-Step programs, even societal laws and regulations. Your greatest teacher, however, will remain the still, small voice within that never shouts, only whispers; never shoves, only nudges. Always, this voice of spirit suggests the wisest course of action. Follow its guidance and your journey will be free of detours, land mines, and spiritual devastation.

Be patient, stumbling pilgrim. You are learning, you are advancing, you are always loved. Peace.

REFLECTION 14

Better Ways of Learning

A stoned motorcyclist recently told me he made a "searching and fearless moral inventory" of himself after slamming into a passing truck, which had left him in a coma for three days. His ego's inability to let go of addiction had propelled him to the brink of death. Yet he returned a new man, with a greatly heightened sense of humility and, soon after joining Narcotics Anonymous, an infusion of support.

Do such wake-up calls always wake us up? No, they do not. One of my former tenants, for example, became despondent when her stoned lover killed himself while recklessly flying his single-engine plane. She, in turn, increased her use of drugs and booze, and later tried to kill herself with a shotgun. But she only managed to blow off her arm and shoulder. Despite this second wake-up call, and the ever-present reminder of a prosthetic arm, she kept indulging her twin addictions. When last I heard from her, she was still an addict.

Before consciously deciding to recover, many of us embrace a trial-and-error method of learning, forcefully confronting ourselves and attempting to learn from raw and sometimes violent experiences. On a subconscious level, we have *chosen* this often painful course of instruction because others have proven ineffective. Behind today's soaring divorce rates and the brutal crimes and turmoil in our city streets—indeed, behind all the violence that permeates our society—are individuals choosing by trial and error to learn the universe's fundamental laws.

Once we have started on the Twelve Steps to recovery, however, we no longer need such drastic wake-up calls, for we have gotten the message. We have discovered that we are an addict, have admitted it to ourselves, and have turned ourselves over to God's care. Now we can learn by attending support groups, and by listening as others with similar addictions admit their mistakes and integrate their lessons. We can learn by reading books as well, and by participating in workshops and watching television shows, such as *Leaving Las Vegas,* that focus on the darker side of society. The more we confront human denial and its graphic consequences, the better versed we become in our *own* destructive dynamics. Broadened by such experience and knowledge, we become equipped to override the shame and low self-esteem that were driving our addiction, and to be more self-realized human beings.

Always, our most profound learning comes from the quiet voice of our higher self, which steers us away from costly mistakes into currents that challenge but do not overwhelm us. Some people call this source of wisdom our sixth sense, or intuition. Whatever terminology you adopt, understand this is the guidance that cannot be heard by a wanderer still in the grip of addiction. Having heard it yourself, welcome its return from a long "spiritual sabbatical," and honor its wisdom as the best reason of all to continue your recovery.

REFLECTION 15

The Middle Path

Many pilgrims, upon extricating themselves from the clutches of addiction, soon begin to wonder what it means to lead a full, somewhat enlightened life. Having great wealth, or even enough money to live comfortably, does not lead to a full life; on the contrary, accruing money and possessions is simply another addiction. We lead a full, awakened existence when we are functional enough to both see the "big picture" and focus on solving day-to-day problems, to maintain close contact with our Higher Power and also deepen our involvement with other people while working, volunteering, parenting, or partnering. As humanity evolves, more of us will live this enlightened existence.

Getting there is not as difficult as it may sound. According to the Buddha, the shortest route to the summit of divine perfection is the middle path. Typically, the middle path lacks the spectacular thrills of euphoria as well as the soul-deadening trances of mundane immersions. Located midway between these two extremes, this path home to spirit is characterized by balance, and those who tread its turf are happy. Conversely, inner happiness is an excellent indication that one is walking an enlightened path.

Our strides along this path can feel puzzling or mysterious until we note their far-reaching effects. For this, we must remember that one lifetime does not determine the ultimate progress of a soul any more than one day represents the full measure of a person's life. Indeed, many lifetimes of effort are needed to evolve an individual whose soul glistens and sparkles through the garb of personality. It takes eons of polishing to produce this wonder for others to see, admire, and emulate.

Mike

—A Member of Narcotics Anonymous—

There's no excuse for why I'm a narcotics addict. I grew up in Minnesota, where I had plenty of advantages. I was one of six kids in a family with two parents. Although we didn't have a lot of money, there was enough for me to own a motorcycle and a snowmobile at the age of eleven. We lived in a small town, with no locks on the doors. The milkman would walk right in and put fresh milk in the refrigerator.

But despite our normal middle-class existence, seven of our eight family members are in recovery programs. My dad was a raging alcoholic from the time I was born, but as a kid I never knew it. Everything seemed pretty ordinary at home, even if every once in a while Dad felt it necessary to sleep in the bathroom. My older brother and sister were into heavy partying at a very young age, and I started looking around when I was ten. I saw that when the old folks partied they drank, and with a couple of drinks in them they were a lot of fun to be around—especially Dad. A few drinks more, though, and I'd feel squirmy and embarrassed. It was a feeling I often had at these scenes; the drinking was disgusting and revolting, yet strangely compelling as well.

Sometime after my eleventh birthday, I told myself, "I'm going to smoke pot, because it's fun and my friends say it's okay." Before long, I was getting loaded every day. By the time I graduated from high school, I was a full-blown addict. I had dropped out of all sports and into the counter culture, getting loaded on one thing or another every day and beginning to lose my dignity and self-respect. I knew I had a drug problem, and at times I tried to quit, but the thought of abstaining from *all* drugs had never crossed my mind.

Basically, this train was headed for a dead end. Time after

time, I would end up totally toxic, drugged, insane, broken up, and humiliated. I would say, "I've got to get my stuff together," and I would stop using this and this and use only that and that, staying pretty much on the up and up. Then I'd get myself breathing and pumped up, and crash into the wall again. That was the mode I was in when my sister, bless her soul, saw me smelling bad, hair all greasy, just trying to show up for each new day. And she said, "Do you think your life is becoming unmanageable? Do you want to go to a meeting with me?"

So off we went to a Narcotics Anonymous (NA) meeting. With only 1,000 NA groups in existence, it seemed a fluke that there was one in my area; that was my first surprise. The second was that stumbling into the meeting was like slipping into a suddenly safe space. I still remember a guy there saying, "No matter what I do, it's like I have to jack off five times a day." And I recall telling myself, "These NA people have honesty." I knew that here I could be myself—a guy who humiliated himself all the time, who tried to move through life in a shoe that didn't fit, who had no dignity or self-respect. All that changed when I used for the last time, which was twenty years ago.

Here's what I did. First, I made a commitment with my sponsor to go to a meeting at least once a week. Second, I held to it, sometimes going every day. Why? Because NA was my friend and offered me something I could feel in my heart. It also cleared a path that led me—a cynical kind of guy who didn't put much truck in this God thing—to believe in God. Everything people were saying about God when I was growing up turned out to be a bunch of hogwash the moment NA gave me permission to link "spirituality" with my heart and mind. I still see it that way. Every day, I earnestly turn my will and my life over to God. I say, "Okay, God, I don't know where we're headed now, but you're driving. Let's go."

My twenty-year birthday of sobriety has done something special for me. Love just pours out of the woodwork. People tell me, "Mike, I appreciate you. You mean something to me.

You've made a contribution to my life." And I realize that without NA this sleazy, lying little dope fiend from the sticks of Minnesota would never have the kind of life I've got. It's not all roses, but it *is* truthful. And it helps me learn how to be free— one day at a time.

Truth

*In telling another person the truth of my life,
I free myself of guilt and open to new possibilities.*

It is one thing to take a fearless inventory of our shortcomings, and quite another to tell a room full of people the raw truth about our misguided lives, which is what Step Five suggests we do. At my first AA meetings, I was amazed to hear so many personal secrets pour out of my fellow alcoholics. Yet listening to their stories encouraged me to be more honest, both with myself and with others. When my turn came, I looked around the room, felt the sanctity of a confessional booth, and while speaking, suddenly realized I was talking not to all these people but to God—the Higher Power in us all. That discovery gave me the courage to open up and share the darkest parts of myself. Then, following the release of these shadowy secrets, fresh thoughts took their place, leading to an immediate sense of renewal. As my recovery progressed, listening to the experiences of others became humbling and fortifying.

A stiff-necked Presbyterian, I felt greatly relieved to admit my most awful secrets to God, myself, and others. At the time, I had no idea religious sacraments could play a leading role in our spiritual development; all I knew was that I was reminded of a Catholic confessional. Speaking to this room full of people felt as safe as talking to a priest—

I could tell the truth and not be betrayed. After all, my words were falling on God's ears. As time went on, I could see how truth-telling opened me to a stream of peer compassion and to a refreshing sense of humor about life. It was a flow I attributed partly to the fact that in AA there is a confidentiality pact and a basic decency about giving and receiving.

In essence, Step Five allows us to unwind *without fear of retribution.* Having been coiled up for so long in addiction and obsessive thinking, many of us are as tight as tops. And now at last, we are free to talk about past incidents that may have frightened us. When we shine light on our darkness in this way, it loses its potency. At this point, many recovering addicts turn to the Serenity Prayer: "God grant me the serenity to accept the things I cannot change, the courage to change the things I can, and the wisdom to know the difference."

This is also the stage where, tapping into our renewed link to intuition, we select a sponsor. Every group has worthy candidates to choose from, and our task is to pick someone we can trust implicitly, then unquestioningly turn ourselves over to their care and guidance. It helps to remember that whatever our addiction is, others have experienced it, too. Sponsors, for their part, know that what was lovingly given to them can be polished by giving it to another with equal love.

Step Five delves into the forgiveness and relief we feel when we finally confess our terrors and wrongdoings, and it examines the components of healthy truth-telling. Reflection 16, "How to Forgive Yourself," is a practical lesson in the nature of sin and the release of guilt. Reflection 17, "Love, Evil, and Inertia," explores the factors that allow us to speak so freely in Twelve-Step meetings. Reflection 18, "Honesty As a Standard," shows how each courageous act of self-forgiveness, as well as each connection made with our Higher Power, elevates all of humanity.

REFLECTION 16

How to Forgive Yourself

The Navajo people believe that humans are at times possessed, that dark winds blow through them, driving them to perform acts that are out of sync with the forces of the universe. The Navajo way is not to encourage such individuals to punish themselves or have society lock them away, but rather to restore them to *hozho*—balance and harmony. Dark winds, it is said, can arise suddenly and carry away our good intentions, such as when a high-spirited friend tells us, "Come on, one beer won't hurt you," and we override our decision not to drink. Or when we accept an invitation to do a line of coke, or respond to a seductive glance or touch, or decide to bet on a "sure thing."

Addicts in recovery can easily lose out to the strong winds of greed, lust, selfishness, miscalculation, and persistent demands. At such times, it is important to avoid judging our actions and to restore ourselves to harmony by reaffirming the presence of God's will in our lives. In passing a sentence on ourselves—or on another, for that matter—we are acting out of self-will and hence separating ourselves from our Higher Power. Judgment, the path of separation, is a sure road back to addiction. Allowing the healing power of remorse and humility to cleanse our self-inflicted wounds, on the other hand, summons the God force within us to restore our balance.

How, then, do we release our guilt? We do this by first confessing our transgression to another person, and then praying for forgiveness and letting the Great Spirit heal us. While praying, we remain honest and humble, accepting with faith the comfort of being in God's care. In this way, we turn the matter over to God. Those who continue to dwell on their sins have not released them. Worse, those who take perverse delight in past transgressions often become caught in another addictive syndrome until, with God's helping hand, they can finally be purged of both the guilt and the precipitating action.

It helps to remember that transgressions are also emblematic of saints and prophets. Did not Moses kill another man in anger, and David send his lover's husband off to war? Did not Joseph's brothers toss him into a pit and leave him for dead? Did not Paul help destroy fellow Jews who professed to be Christians? Having erred, each of these people prayed for forgiveness, were instantly pardoned, and went on to serve God as grateful, powerful way-showers.

Transgressions impede human progress only if we pause in dismay at their intrusion into our consciousness, and waste precious time berating ourselves over them. To err is human; to forgive, divine; and to forgive quickly, everlasting. Just as a branding iron need only touch the hide to leave its mark, so too can you learn your lessons quickly and move rapidly on.

REFLECTION 17

Love, Evil, and Inertia

At support group meetings everywhere, I am heartened each time I hear the searching and dauntless stories people tell about their lives as addicts. What was once considered "airing dirty laundry" is now a cleansing experience—for the listeners as well as the speakers. But what allows these people to speak with such candor? And what draws forth the quiet support and deep empathy they receive for the often raw details they unfalteringly reveal?

Behind the scenes, there are three forces at work. The first is *love*—the primitive longing of one seeking to join with another in a more perfect union. Love motivates people, animals, plants, minerals, even molecules to become part of a greater whole. At the core of this dynamic attraction is a yearning for spiritual perfection, or completion. In support groups we are united by our love of God and self, and by welcoming into our spiritual fold those who seek recovery from their God-severing addictions.

The second operative factor is an awareness of *evil*—forces of chaos and separation that fight against evolution, perfection, and oneness. Evil drives us to reject opportunities for growth, for forgiveness, and for greater community with others. One of its greatest instruments is the ego, which insists on adherence to human will rather than God's will; another of its instruments is addiction, which disconnects us from our better self and the love of God and family, leaving us with unmanageable lives. Program members reckon with the force of evil every day. They also recognize its face on those entering recovery, and offer help in eradicating it.

In her book *Shadow and Evil in Fairy Tales*, the great Jungian psychologist Maria-Louise von Franz concluded, after studying the collective wisdom of thousands of fairy tales from around the world, that when we meet evil on the road, we should not try to redeem it or convert it, but rather kill it. Similarly, while there is much empathy expressed in recovery support groups, there is little patience for the evil that drives addiction. When it comes to this force, "tough love" is the reigning response.

The third factor contributing to the atmosphere of honesty, support, and empathy is an understanding of *inertia*—the indisposition to exertion or change. Inertia has us walking through a jungle and refusing to grab a hanging vine to swing out of the path of a rampaging tiger. It also has us recognizing our addiction yet not moving into recovery from it, or refusing the counsel of our support group. It often rears its head at the pivotal point of decision making, where we are about to either refuse recovery or embrace it with resolve and vigorous action. This is another condition that those in support groups know well and can help move others through, if they so choose, into sobriety.

An understanding of love, evil, and inertia is what will meet you at the threshold of sharing your truth. It is what informs those who are waiting to help you take the next step. As such, it will either propel you into recovery or, if you lack resolve and threaten the sobriety of others, show you to the door.

REFLECTION 18

Honesty As a Standard

Mythologies call to mind a time of human innocence, an era before our so-called fall from grace. It was an age when peace and harmony ruled the planet, when there were no misdeeds, and hence no occasions to speak of betrayal or treachery. Unconditional love flowed from person to person universally. Now, although we have walked out of Eden into the darkness of human travail, individuals such as St. Francis of Assisi in the West and Ramakrishna in the East reveal the still-present potential to live in grace.

If we could ask these revered saints to name the human trait they honored above all else, they would no doubt say *honesty*—the basis of trust. Have we not seen what dishonesty does in our relationships with others? Can we even conceive of a relationship with our Higher Power marred by lies and deceit? Honesty at every level is the ideal to hold to in moving ourselves and our society into a new era of spiritual awakening.

To begin, we must be honest with ourselves about our transgressions, then share them with others in our support group. After revealing to others our horrendous failings, it is a simple matter to be honest in all our dealings, from paying taxes to honoring our commitments to family and community. Imagine what the world would be like if, after we moved naturally forward, everybody followed our example and held honesty as their absolute standard.

It may seem a stretch for some people to elevate our deeds to such heights, especially those who think of addicts as the dregs of society. Yet we who have overcome deep-seated addictions walk the same path as St. Paul and other sinners who have seen the light and reformed themselves. And what moves a society to new heights is not the politicians and religious leaders, but rather every individual dealing honestly with their failings and struggling to reclaim their higher potential with each act of self-forgiveness, each connection to their Higher Power, each day of sobriety.

So, the next time you step in front of a recovery group to confess your shortcomings, think of the impact you are having. Realize that with each honest assessment you share, you are contributing to the transformation and elevation of humans everywhere.

Jeff

—A Member of Debtors Anonymous—

I'm a compulsive debtor, a self-pauper, which is by definition an underearner. For a self-pauper, it's year after year of just scraping by. You're always incurring debt and never getting ahead, unable to pay your own way, forever borrowing from family and friends to make ends meet. I always borrowed with good intentions, but I never paid anyone back. I wanted to, of course, but I never managed to earn more than rent money. Over time, this led me to a deep depression—a state of not caring anymore. It was like being drugged out, in terms of having nothing to look forward to and no life for myself.

My turning point came when I decided to do whatever it took to get out of debt. I began by going to a Debtors Anonymous (DA) meeting and, right there in that room, surrendering to my Higher Power. I was told, "The Higher Power must be something outside of yourself, even if it's a shoe, so make this program your Higher Power if you can't reach up to God." And that's what I did. I made the program my Higher Power and then later connected it to God.

That day at DA, I committed myself to the program and started doing everything they said. When they said to do service, I did service. When they said to keep money and records, I kept them. When they said to work and earn wages, I took whatever job I could find. At first, I came to the meetings angry, hating the drudgery they put me through, sometimes almost crawling there. Yet every time, I left with a gift: relief and fellowship. I went from having no life to realizing I would never be alone again.

With recovery came better and better employment, and increased income. I now have more self-esteem, I'm closer to my son, and I'm even solvent. For nearly ten years I've incurred no unsecured debt. In fact my debt, which was $13,000, has shrunk to $4,000, and one day soon it will be gone. I don't even think about it anymore.

Phase Three recovery of DA is "going for your vision." Now that you've got your recovery, you're solvent, and you're not debting, you get to check in and see what you want for yourself. My vision was to have a wonderful house. So I did the research and prayed—always, you do the footwork not knowing what the result might be. Then one day, a friend in real estate walked me through the area of town where I wanted to live, and there it was: my house. A few weeks later, I discovered that a clause in my grandfather's trust left me money for real estate, and it was enough to let me buy my dream house. It's like God steps up and moves through your life when you have the courage to take action on your own behalf.

Courage

I used to draw false courage from my addiction.
I now ask my Higher Power to remove my character
defects so I may experience true courage.

Step Six is one of the most challenging stages in the recovery process. Now we must be ready and willing to correct our character defects, some of which are deep-seated and resistant to reform. This means, among other things, weeding out the rationalizations that for years have supported our addiction. Stealing money or merchandise from an unsuspecting employer may help pay the rent each month, but no longer can we attempt to justify these acts by telling ourselves, "I'm just borrowing it" or "They'll never miss it." Nor can we excuse casual or extramarital sex by saying, "I'm just playing around. It doesn't mean anything." Such justifications only reinforce the lack of self-worth and integrity that lie at the root of our addiction.

Can we be honest enough to acknowledge these tenacious character flaws and offer them up to our Higher Power? Stripping ourselves of these defects enables us to keep our addiction in check; and indeed, experience has shown that we cannot live soberly while clinging to them. The expression uttered in countless recovery meetings is, "It's time to come clean." And in coming clean we derive courage.

My most persistent failing was the loose moral conduct I exhibited while drinking. Although I knew it was degrading to have sex with women I didn't care about, I did it anyway. Then when I began to work the Sixth Step, I had to decide if I was willing to release my desire for a woman I regularly engaged in sex. This, for me, was a big test. How did I summon the courage to let go of my lust? I prayed for the strength to overcome this obstacle on my path to recovery. Prayer, I have discovered, helps us release desires of all sorts. And when we pray to our Higher Power to remove character defects, they will most certainly be eradicated.

While working this Step, I had to give myself over to God *completely*. No longer could I be content dipping my big toe in the pool to test the water, for it was time to go straight to the deep end and jump in. During this stage of recovery, half-measures will not work; we either surrender our will or we don't. Fortunately, the humble act of surrendering can take place anywhere—at work, on a park bench, in the shower, or in St. Patrick's Cathedral—and is bound to evoke a powerful response. As Sister Ignatia would say, with an Irish gleam in her eyes, "God *loves* to hear from strangers."

We are moving steadily forward. In Step Four, we took a moral inventory of ourselves, turning on a light in the darkened recesses of the soul. In Step Five, we revealed our most gnarled impediments to recovery. Now, we must actively overcome our paralysis by releasing them. The buck stops *here*.

Step Six has us mobilize our resources for action. Reflection 19 takes us on "An Adventure in Self-Discovery," where we identify the "self" to whom we owe our allegiance. Reflection 20, "How 'Easy' Does It," explores the functions of time in the journey to true selfhood. Reflection 21, "Setting and Reaching a Goal," explains how to uncover our goals and cultivate the singleness of purpose needed to attain them.

An Adventure in Self-Discovery

In turning to a Higher Power capable of removing our character defects and freeing us from addiction, we begin to identify with a power greater than our addicted selves. Through its promptings, we eventually realize that we are endowed with a higher self—a soul—and that one of our main tasks is to elevate our consciousness so that we *become* this higher self, for it is our true self. To empower us in this mission, AA members are given, after specific periods of sobriety, a medallion bearing the inscription "To thine own self be true."

Interestingly, the true self is no stranger to us. Before launching ourselves into human form, we engage in careful preparation and "soul searching" with our spiritual guides—a process that may be somewhat akin to working with sponsors in a Twelve-Step program. Together with our guides, we draw up plans to enrich our immortal soul with fresh experiences, additional challenges, and new ways to become more perfect and godlike. Past failings are there to be redeemed and past successes to be augmented; in addition, previously untapped avenues of growth are charted for the continued evolution of our soul.

To gradually uncover the true self, now buried within our core, requires sustained effort. It is said that the stronger the person, the more arduous the challenge. And addictions, because they sever us from our higher self, become battlefields where we fight for our redemption. Faithful, diligent, and dogged adherence to Twelve-Step programs can quicken the desired contact by subduing the soul-severing addictions. It may take years to penetrate the layers of misconception, error, and surface distraction that surround the addictive self like a fog. Still, just as the prodigal son returns home much to his father's joy, so does self find self and heartily rejoice in the reunion.

First, however, we must learn to *recognize* the genuine self. Recognition requires us to cut through all soul-deadening experiences, messages from false prophets, and sensual distractions, in search of the pure light of self that shines from the Great Spirit. Always, although the path may be dark and twisted, we can rely on the guidance of our spiritual helpers and on that spark within to light our way.

Having discovered the true self in the temple of the body, we will regard our present circumstances with fresh interest and a new detachment. Our consciousness will simultaneously enlarge to embrace an awareness of this immortal self as it evolves within the limited world of the senses during the human passage from birth to death.

Such a goal is the desire of many yet the prize of only a few. May you be among them.

REFLECTION 20

How "Easy" Does It

Many recovering addicts are impatient with the time it takes for order to emerge from the chaos they have long endured. The best antidote to this impatience is the advice that an AA old-timer will give a newcomer: "You didn't get this way overnight. Take it slow. Easy does it." To offset his own impatience, the newcomer might establish a climate of acceptance by saying: "Here I am, God. I've made a real mess of things. I'm flying blind. I need your help." In the silence that follows such an admission—which is more likely to be in God's time than in the speaker's—he will receive the requested help.

The importance of letting time take its course to create something of lasting value is illustrated in the following story:

> Once upon a time, three dwarfs lived together in a rocky hillside cave in France. Although ridiculed by their peers, these men had turned their backs on city life and had resolved to find peace and contentment living close to nature in the remote countryside. For their livelihood, they compressed the curd of milk into cheese and tended a nearby vineyard owned by a man of wealth.
>
> One day Henri, the eldest of the three dwarfs, came upon a piece of parchment that had been buried in the dark recesses of their cave. After studying it carefully, he discovered that it contained a formula for producing a cheese unknown to the world. What distinguished this recipe from others was the extensive amount of time allotted to maturing the cheese. The dwarfs, deciding to produce this strange cheese, followed the ancient recipe, then stored the vat of mixed ingredients in the recesses of their cave and promptly forgot about it.

As they strolled through the countryside one evening more than a year later, their conversation turned to unusual cheeses, whereupon Henri remembered the cache in the back of their hillside home. After a little searching, he found the vat and unwrapped the cheese before an audience of two curious onlookers. The substance was moldy-looking and had unusual blue veins running through it.

The dwarfs tasted it, then stared at one another in wide-eyed surprise and pleasure: the cheese had a uniquely pungent flavor that reminded them of wine, of sunshine and laughter, of genial good living. So they took a portion of it to market the next day.

When customers passed by their stall, the dwarfs offered them generous samples of their "new" cheese, which became an instant hit with the villagers. Soon its fame spread to Cologne, where a large cheese merchant contacted the three dwarfs and obtained exclusive rights to market their product.

As demand for this delicacy increased, the dwarfs found other methods for producing it. But despite the singular mixture of substances they added, the magic ingredient was always the extended time taken to mature the cheese in the cave environment. The final product, named Roquefort cheese, came to be known and loved throughout the world, and to this day neither its texture nor its flavor has been duplicated elsewhere.

Each of us is born with distinct characteristics that, like the dwarfs' vats of cheese, come together to form a unique creation. A particular "flavor" emerges when our soul's pattern mixes with our inborn physical, mental, and emotional propensities, as well as such environmental influences as family dynamics and socioeconomic factors. And for these various forces to meld and mature into the person our soul has intended, the needed ingredient is time. The more patient we are, the more likely each part of our being will come to expression. After all, a giant oak tree doesn't achieve its great stature in only one season.

Unfortunately, most of us rush the maturation process. We mistakenly believe that we are prepared to accept any assignment, challenge, or opportunity that comes our way—which is our will speaking, rather than God's. How easily we forget that, as King Solomon wrote, "to every thing there is a season, and a time to every purpose under the heaven: a time to be born, and a time to die; a time to plant, and a time to pluck up that which is planted ..." [Ecclesiastes 3:1–2]. When we act prematurely, we are like a young colt that, racing to keep up with its older siblings, fails to jump the fence, injuring itself and possibly limiting its future potential.

How do we know if we are prepared to take action on a particular impulse? By building a "time bridge" where we can pause, reflect, and consult our Higher Power. The final authority in all such decisions should be our soul's prompting. That way, we will be able to harness our energies, develop our talents, govern our will, and master the opportunity as a more complete person. Remember, much misery has come from asking butterflies to emerge prematurely from their cocoons.

Setting and Reaching a Goal

With so many demands calling out for our attention, how can we possibly establish worthy goals, much less attain them? Noted Swiss psychologist Carl Jung said that our feelings guide us in setting valuable goals. It has also been said that "feelings are the soul's whisperings." Listening to our feelings can certainly help us choose appropriate goals in life.

Listening to our feelings, however, is not always easy. At times, it means refusing to be overly influenced by others, including family or friends, a priest or a rabbi. At other times, it requires us to screen out advertisers' pitches claiming that true happiness lies in achieving sparkly white teeth with this toothpaste, driving that sports car, or wearing designer jeans.

Once we have let our feelings prescribe appropriate goals for ourselves, how do we achieve them? One way is by enkindling a fervent desire to, for only flames of passion can deflect the myriad of diversions competing for our attention on a daily basis. Interestingly, the failure to accomplish goals is most often attributed to the distractions of contemporary life, which are nothing other than society's addictions; they draw us away from our pursuit of life-fulfilling objectives to support those of the social order instead. As our world becomes more complex, with cell phones, e-mail, and portable Internet devices, we must be especially careful of all such habituating influences.

In addition to stoking up desire and bypassing societal temptations, we can persevere toward our chosen goals by symbolically reminding ourselves of them through photographs, paintings, or special words or phrases. The image of a snow-capped mountain is a good visual reminder of moving toward a summit of any sort. Some people prefer a photograph of a holy person (Gandhi is a favorite in ashrams) or a brilliant scientist (Albert Einstein is popular in student dorms), or a portrait of a lesser-known admired person. Others will display an inspiring quotation. When we consistently envision what we wish to accomplish, it eventually materializes. Donald Trump, perhaps aware of this spiritual law, constructs intricate models of his proposed buildings so that he can visualize their completion.

Ultimately, to keep our focus and see our way through to the end, we also need the gift of courage from our Higher Power. Without tuning in to our still, small voice, we can be easily pulled off course. Hearing it, however, we are able to maintain singleness of purpose by marshaling the forces of determination, divinely inspired will, persistence, and optimism, eventually achieving our goals. Other contributing factors are constant prayer, an attitude of humility, and gratitude for the opportunities and challenges that invite us to move forward.

Elizabeth

—A Member of Alcoholics Anonymous—

I started drinking in high school, along with all my friends. We lived in a small town in South Dakota where there was nothing going on, so a lot of us ended up drinking and doing drugs. I didn't have much of a problem in school, but when I was eighteen I married someone who drank every day. To keep up with him, I needed to learn how to drink better. So I "practiced" until I could hold as much alcohol as he and his friends. Even though I had at least one drink a day for ten or fifteen years, things didn't often get out of control; but when they did, they got worse and worse.

What ended my drinking was a big fight I had with my husband during a New Year's Eve party at our house. Afterward, I was cleaning the mess downstairs and he was upstairs in bed. I went up, pulled back the covers, and said, "Get up. I want to talk to you." Not till then did I notice he had a shotgun next to him. He sat up and put it to my head. "Just pull the trigger," I said. "Kill me and get it over with. I don't want to live. It just isn't worth it anymore." He laughed and told me, "No, I won't do that. But here's the gun. It's okay if you do it to yourself."

He left me there and went downstairs to the kids' room. So I put the gun to my head and pulled the trigger, but it didn't go off. As I ducked into the closet for more shells, I had a spiritual awakening. God came to me and said, "Do you want to live or die?" As if in response, I headed downstairs, opened the back door, shot the gun off in the yard, and threw it on a nearby snowbank.

I proceeded to drink round-the-clock for the next five days. Then in another moment of clarity I heard a voice say, "If you're going to live, you need to quit drinking. You cannot drink and live."

So I quit drinking and got super sick and crazy as hell. I would go to a bar with friends, order tomato juice, and tell them, "I'm not drinking." Then I'd laugh hysterically. Eventually, I went to my doctor and asked for tranquilizers, because I was too wound up to eat or sleep; in fact, I was awake twenty-four hours a day. My doctor said, "If I give you tranquilizers, you'll just switch from one addiction to another." He told me to go to Alcoholics Anonymous (AA).

The meeting was in a hospital lounge, and to get there you had to go through the lobby and past the nurse's station, which meant that all the people you passed knew where you were going. When I came home, I told my husband, who out of embarrassment refused to let me continue. My doctor, however, insisted, saying, "Elizabeth, you are free to do whatever you want. Go to AA." So I did.

At the meetings, I met a woman who took me to an outpatient treatment center in Rapid City. There I lived in a halfway house, where people took care of me. I still wasn't eating or sleeping, even though it had been a while since I'd quit drinking. There, too, I was introduced to the Twelve Steps. I had to do at least the first four while in treatment.

That was twenty-two years ago, and I haven't had a drink since. What's odd is that although I know I'm an alcoholic, it hasn't been helpful to tell others. In fact, I had to move from South Dakota just to avoid the label, because the locals there look down on alcoholics; they think we're bad people. I found that if you go to a job interview and say, "I'm a recovering alcoholic," they won't hire you. Even now, while socializing with coworkers, I feel isolated. When they ask why I won't join them for a glass of wine, I say I'm allergic to it. Inside, though, I feel deeply humbled.

Humility

*I give up my evasive actions and game-playing,
and summon the courage to scatter all roadblocks
that have prevented me from overcoming my addiction.*

Jesus' act of washing the apostles' feet at the Last Supper suggests that no matter what our worldly position or net worth may be, we serve a higher purpose. In doing so, and in graciously accepting the rule of God over self, we demonstrate humility. People who sincerely allow God's will to work through them tend not to shout it from the rooftops; rather, in their quiet ways they exhibit humility. Pious and overly earnest individuals, on the other hand, take great pride in displaying their *false* humility. In other words, if you think you have humility you probably don't.

This point is illustrated by a story I once heard about a new member of a recovery support group. The man went so far as to rehearse his first talk to the group before a mirror, making sure his inflections were just right. After addressing the group, he anxiously awaited their comments. One member after another stood up and responded to certain points he had made. Then a sweet young woman added, "Another thing I liked about your talk was your humility."

"I was hoping you'd notice it," the man replied earnestly.

Recognizing in all humility that our self-importance is ineffectual, and that we can't "go it alone," signals a dramatic change in attitude.

Since childhood, we have been taught the ethic of self-determination—of standing up for ourselves and not letting anyone or anything knock us down. By asserting our intelligence and willpower, we have learned, we can master any problem. Yet here we are faced with an addiction that no amount of willpower can vanquish.

It is a truly humbling experience for a politican, sports star, industrial leader, or man of the cloth to be arrested on a drinking-while-intoxicated charge and placed in the cooler. Suddenly, if they listen closely, they might hear their higher self whispering, "*Let go* to win." At that point, they may acknowledge their powerlessness and humbly ask for help. Or they may later attend an AA meeting and hear, "Let go and let God," and then humbly align their will with God's. It can be a great joy for anyone addicted to self-importance to unload their loneliness, discovering that help is only a tiny surrender away.

Whenever I am grappling with a difficult situation, I try to go straight to God. In prayer, I turn the burden of my self-determination over to my Higher Power, all the while remaining an active participant. Instead of praying, "May thy will *be done*," I say, "*I do* thy will." This is my promise to God, and to help fulfill it I ask God for strength. For example, I recently realized I'd been overreacting to my wife's concern about my driving. Bothered by her anxiety and convinced that we were driving at a safe speed, I often ended up yelling at her. One day, instead of yelling I prayed; right away, I received the message that I should merely thank her for her vigilance and slow down. I took the advice, which not only improved the atmosphere in the car and in our relationship but also taught me that screaming, "I'm right!" will never foster peace and harmony.

Step Seven separates the men from the boys, the women from the girls. Although we may bluff our way through a support group meeting, carefully disguising our character defects, they will continue to feed our addiction. If our goal is sobriety, we must humbly ask God to remove these obstructions to our full recovery. In Step Six we announced our readiness to have our defects removed; now we invite their removal. Reflection 22, "How a 'Happening' Can Happen," demonstrates ways to prepare for a union with spirit. Reflection 23, "How Our Prayers Are Answered," sheds light on prayer as the ultimate vehicle of surrender.

REFLECTION 22

How a "Happening" Can Happen

Humility helps us advance from a negative lifestyle to a positive one. So it is that humbly asking God, in whatever way comes naturally, to remove our shortcomings leads to a resounding, almost palpable victory over our addiction. St. Augustine, after thirty-two years of wild living, experienced such an epiphany in a garden. There the sound of a child's singing touched his heart, signaling his conversion to a more saintly life.

Humility also helped a young Hessian soldier named Gregory who, during a lull in battle, entered a German chapel and headed straight for the cruxifix behind the altar. There he fell to his knees, begged forgiveness for his dastardly ambush of enemy soldiers, then asked that God's vision and wisdom guide his future actions. Gregory later became king—a leader known to have ruled his subjects with compassion. This story illustrates a singular fact of human existence: *One golden moment of spiritual union can rearrange the loose blocks of our lives, producing a configuration that is better suited to God's purpose for us.*

How do such spiritual breakthroughs come about? Can they be ordered, like an entrée on a dinner menu? Hardly, for such a "happening" originates with God's grace and occurs only when all is in readiness. We can, however, prepare for it in the following ways:

- By being willing to change our habits and align our actions more closely with divine law. We make this change by attending meetings and walking the Steps.

- By observing God's will for us rather than our own. This we do by creating an opening through which our character defects can be removed.

- By renewing our dedication to enact God's will daily, if not hourly, through meditation, prayer, and firm resolve.

It is no wonder relatively few of us remain on this path! Worldly distractions and the glorification of ego are exceedingly alluring, often obliterating the rewards available through serving God's will. To stay on the path to a spiritual breakthrough, we cannot be blinded by the blitz. Instead, we need to keep intact our own will, body, mind, and purpose, and then live in sacred preparedness for the transformative moment of union.

We are the captain of our team. We call together the players, set the tone and caliber of our offering, and humbly present it to our Higher Power, not to some distant magician who performs sleight-of-hand miracles. It is we who bring forth what we desire and ardently pray for. Why is this so? Because once we have linked our intent with God's power, our potential becomes limitless.

REFLECTION 23

How Our Prayers Are Answered

What happens when we pray? We direct our energies toward the fulfillment of a specific desire. Simultaneously, our request releases energy particles in much the same way a television's cathode-ray tube sends out a stream of electrons that the human retina interprets as an image. In the case of prayer, the energy particles are received by our higher self, God or God's intermediaries, and a variety of other forces. These energy receptors either manifest the desired outcome or reinterpret it to serve a greater good.

For example, if a prayer is directed toward the recovery of a woman hospitalized with a grave illness, the prayer's energy is instantly received by the woman's spiritual guides, as well as the nurses and doctors attending her. The atmosphere surrounding her also becomes charged with its energy. If it is in the woman's highest good, her doctor might come up with a more accurate diagnosis or a more effective treatment plan, leading to her rapid recovery. Of course, the energy might also be used by the woman's guides to help release her from this plane of existence.

It is important to remember that *man proposes* and *God disposes*. God's disposition became clearly apparent in the outcome of World War II, after many German people had prayed fervently for victory. Their prayers may in fact have energized the outcome that served the greater good. If a prayer is for something less specific, such as the enlightenment of government leaders, the betterment of society, or the easing of international tensions, the energy transmitted operates in much the same way.

Praying for one's enemies or for those who misuse their power is the highest form of prayer, as Jesus pointed out in his Sermon on the Mount. Such prayer can help reverse an enemy's otherwise intractable antagonism and restore equilibrium. With the restoration of balance, they are apt to feel more positive about their former opponent—resulting in the reestablishment of harmony and the answer to another prayer.

Knowing that our prayers are not always answered in the way we wish, we may ask, "If I might not get what I want, why pray at all?" Our wants, we must remember, are based on our limited perspectives; we cannot possibly see the grand scope of our lives or what is best for the common good. Our task is simply to pray, for in doing so we provide energy that activates the universal forces. This concept is poignantly illustrated in God's answer to the query of a righteous man who led a deprived existence. On his deathbed, the righteous man asks God why his life was so divested of wealth and resources. He is then shown a room with all of life's riches, and told that he never prayed for anything. As the British poet Alfred Lord Tennyson wrote, "More things are wrought by prayer / Than this world dreams of."

To pray for our own well-being is invariably beneficial. To pray for the good of another is to hold hands with spirit. It is also a way to thank our Higher Power for loving us. Further, it adds to the stream of conscious will for good and desire for perfection that are essential to spirit's plan for us. Ultimately, when we pray for another, we are helped in return, for in keeping with God's law in action such prayers are answered at their source.

Beyond clinical treatment or support group meetings, you have the universe's greatest power at your command: prayer from your heart to God's. Throughout human history this force has transformed the most overwhelming despair into fresh hope, victory, and happiness.

Emily

—A Member of Codependents Anonymous—

I entered Codependents Anonymous (CoDA) after I had been sober for a number of years. As a child, I was sexually abused by my father and mother, as well as other family members; it was an extremely dysfunctional, sadistic family. What I found in my recovery was that I was free from alcohol, free from drugs, and free from compulsive sexual behavior, but something was missing: I wasn't able to have a healthy relationship.

One of my problems was that I made other people my Higher Power, giving them the place in my life that really belongs to God. Most recently, I did that with my alcoholic son. We'd been living together for many years, and I thought I was going to bring him into recovery. Instead, I ended up losing ground myself. I dropped out of recovery and became enmeshed with my son, trying to make up for having been an alcoholic and emotionally absent mother. But in walking away from the spiritual path, I gave myself over to hating. I began to hate my parents intensely, extending the fury to everyone around me, and I ended up hating myself most of all. I refused to forgive anyone.

I had an environmental illness and hadn't worked for years. I felt terribly isolated, which is characteristic of co-dependents; we become dependent on another person and look to them to make decisions for us. At one point, my son decided he wanted to commit suicide and I agreed to it, although I knew in my heart it was wrong. There we were in the car, together with the hose attached to the exhaust; it was my son who had to announce, "Maybe we shouldn't do this," and then turn off the engine.

I'd like to say that after that night-boom I embraced CoDA and lived happily ever after. Wrong! I spent another year and a half living with my son's abusive behavior. Codependents let other people treat them badly, and still look to them for decision making. When I did go back to CoDA, eighteen months later, was when my life started to change. As I reestablished a connection with my Higher Power, I got my faith back and started working the program again. Without it, there's no way I'd be alive today.

I can tell you that not being able to forgive will tear you apart. Hatred will eat you alive. It was only two years ago that I found out my mother sexually abused me—and my hatred almost killed me. In CoDA you discover that dysfunctional behavior is learned in your family system and so you have to look at your past. You don't have to live in it, but you do have to look at it honestly. You have to own the feelings that belong to that past. You have to cry the tears and be angry and be afraid, and let it all out. *Then* you can forgive. Step Eight is the portal, but they're *all* needed.

Forgiveness

I now forgive myself and others,
knowing that it will free me
to move ahead with my life.

How do we know when we have injured another person? If we are stoned and smash into a car, our accountability would be obvious. However, there are more subtle forms of personal injury so deeply rooted in our character that we often overlook them: directing unkind words at someone we love, snubbing a friend, being overbearing with a subordinate, or rude to a waiter or cashier. Although Step Eight assists us in addressing major grievances and making amends to those harmed by our thoughts, words, or actions, it also asks us to examine how our unruly temperament can inflict harm. And so in walking this Step, we develop a keen sense of empathy for others.

For instance, I recently cut in front of another driver, unaware that the road was about to suddenly narrow. I could feel the man's anger and almost hear him cursing. As my wife fanned the flames of *my* anger, I exploded into road rage and gave the fellow the finger. I immediately regretted my lapse in decorum, aware that such outbursts drain away precious life forces that can be better used elsewhere. Indeed, one of the secrets of great achievers is their ability to redirect emotional energy to constructive purposes. In the case of addicts, such energy can be used to recover faster, cleaner, and better.

Another factor to consider while venting anger is the "boomerang effect." Send out anger and anger comes back; send out courtesy or love and *that's* what comes back. The willingness to make amends for unleashing an angry impulse thus leads to more than forgiveness and harmony; every injury we inflict deposits some of our life energy in others, and making amends brings it back to us. Our challenge, then, is to compile a thorough list of people we have injured, and then do what we can to apologize—which may mean anything from saying "I'm sorry" to buying a dozen roses. The operative word in this Step is *willingness*. Like prayer, it is an activating principle that sets the healing energy in motion.

Early in my sobriety, I realized that my greatest resentment was losing my father to leukemia when I was ten. Feeling utterly abandoned by his death, I turned my anger toward my widowed mother, challenging her new authority over me. But not until I discovered how much this resentment was harming me did I become willing to forgive him for dying and leaving me fatherless. As if in response, sponsors came into my life to help guide me through recovery. Although these father figures could never replace a father's love, the boomerang effect was much welcomed. My forgiveness had brought fellowship and love back into my life.

Step Eight encourages us to search our souls for all the people we have harmed, and be *willing* to make amends to them in one way or another. In Reflection 24, "First Things First," we see the importance of clearing out our surface debris before attempting to attain spiritual realization. Reflection 25, "The Past Is Over," asks us to examine our old ways of thinking, especially about others. Reflection 26, "The Battle of Wills," shows how forgiveness and the rule of our Higher Power can forestall yet another draining conflict.

REFLECTION 24

First Things First

The first stage of atonement is understanding the emotional basis of our transgressions and those perpetrated against us. Unless we root out the negative feelings, attitudes, and self-justifications that drive our offenses against others, or theirs against us, how can we possibly experience true forgiveness? Too often we pay off debts simply to wipe clean our personal ledger. That's the easy way out, however. If we don't understand *why* we injure others and don't ask God to *remove* each specific cause, we are apt to continue along a path that leads away from recovery.

Our society is predicated on the principle of paying off collective debts with little effort given to soul searching. We pay off American Indian tribes after violating their land; we clean up our oil and chemical spills; we relocate populations exposed to fallout from our nuclear testing; we limit the scope of our war machine to allay future world wars. But have we *learned* from the transgressions? It seems we have only changed the vehicles of destruction: we now allow globalization to drive the indigenous cultures of Central and South America to the brink of extinction; and to protect "our way of life," we permit global warming to melt Arctic ice shelves, whose waters may eventually flood our coastal cities.

What is the flaw that perpetuates these collective misdeeds? It is our disconnection from spirit—our ego drive for self-actualization gauged only in material terms. We cannot experience forgiveness, or be forgiven of our debts, if we turn around and create more debt elsewhere. We know what *that* is: it's an addiction.

Fortunately, the boomerang effect applies on this level as well. The work we do on ourselves as we apologize and turn our will over to our Higher Power, makes it easier for others to do the same. The collective awareness sparked by Twelve-Step programs alone is remarkable. In the last few years program meetings have riveted public attention on many issues, such as spousal abuse and incest, that might not otherwise have been addressed.

Collective atonement is born of personal atonement. And to move in this direction we must first acknowledge the wounds that drive our offensive actions, the emotional morass that clouds our judgment, and the negativity that prevents the spark of spirit from rising within us. Then we can begin to rectify the damage caused by our actions and to release our anger and resentment over past injuries. As it is said in the Bible, we must take care of our human concerns before storming heaven's gates.

The Past Is Over

Success in releasing negative emotional states and making amends for transgressions comes with the ability to free ourselves of the past, which often has a tenacious grip. What chains us to the past? The human brain does, for it establishes with every action a neural pathway that almost compels us to repeat prior behaviors. Also, our school systems' emphasis on memorization keeps us bound to the past—set up, as it is, to award reiteration. Likewise, we endlessly duplicate the "winning" motion in sports, delivering perfect curved arcs at the bowling alley and 300-yard drives on the golf course.

Many of us, consciously or unconsciously, still live in the past. We listen to oldies on the radio, collect cassettes and CDs that catapult us back in time, and reminisce over videos made from decades-old movies. Childhood experiences, as any psychoanalyst will say, are the root causes of our present-day dysfunctions. Our emotional attachments, too, lock us in the past. So it seems that those of us who do not free ourselves of the past are bound to repeat it, continually replaying our old grievances and transgressions. While it is true that the past also contains endearing memories of loved ones, respected teachers, and star athletes who continue to motivate us, it is the *present* moment that invites spirit to invigorate new actions and directions. The test is to constantly review any content arising from the past and to consciously welcome whatever elevates us while dismissing all that drags us down.

Consciousness is the key to resisting old patterns that fail to serve new growth. In a world seething with change, it is incumbent upon us to stop repeating old mistakes and to carefully select from the past only the morsels that *contribute to a new beginning* for ourselves and humanity. As we take more responsibility for our actions and make amends, the atmosphere around us and in the world will brighten with hope, humor, and the fresh breeze of spiritual awareness.

REFLECTION 26

The Battle of Wills

For many of us, life has become a constant struggle, a battle of wills against an endless array of adversaries bent on frustrating our desires or undermining our supremacy in whatever arena we have staked out. Some would attribute the resulting agony to the "human condition" or the "survival of the fittest." Previous generations, often accepting this struggle as a fact of life, passed on the attitude that "life is a battle royal" and "you'd better get yours before they get you." What a far cry this is from Christ's admonishment to "love one another" and to "do unto others as you would have them do unto you"—doctrines many of us preach while acting out our survivalist roles.

In intimate relationships, where love should reign supreme, we often find the most grueling battle of wills. Partners slipping out of harmony with each other will at first engage in minor skirmishes to win a strategic piece of ground without firing a shot. The clashes may be sparked by an irritating attitude or a habit that grates on the other's nerves. Perhaps the sexual union is less than desirable.

As the hour of open warfare approaches, the two combatants prepare their lists of complaints and recriminations. Invariably, the forces enter into mortal combat. First, one side airs a complaint: "You work too much, never do anything around the house, and expect me to manage the children." Then the other carries the battle forward: "It's the overtime that's going to pay for the children's college education." After a draw of this sort, both sides regroup and come back with more personal grievances, bringing up feelings of abandonment, ingratitude, and inadequacy.

Intimate relationships flush out our deepest and darkest fears. Once these have come to light, we can resolve them; often, however, we continue to project them onto our partner. Similar scenarios unfold with coworkers, neighbors, and children as we try to impose our will on them or get what we want from them.

It is this clash of wills that has driven many of us into addiction, striving to blunt the anxieties and other unnerving feelings they evoke. The best way out of this imbroglio is through forgiveness, which helps us see ourselves and others more clearly. Turning conflicts over to our Higher Power, we will find, can effectively bring peace and harmony to our relationships.

I once read an interview with Peter Caddy, cofounder of the Findhorn Community in Scotland, where a large group of people had gathered to farm plots of hopelessly depleted loose sandy soil by working with nature spirits. Their extraordinary success brought incredulous scientists, agricultural experts, and curious others to these windblown dunes. The reporter, noticing the variety of people—young and old from diverse nations—asked Caddy how they settled disputes. He told the reporter that they never had any, that everybody sat and meditated on an issue until they were all of one mind, which usually happened fairly quickly.

Setting this formula into action in our personal relationships, as well as in community gatherings ranging from PTA meetings to United Nations conferences, we would see more constructive work in the world and less petty squabbling. Often, the action that moves an agenda up to this level is, forgiving ourselves and others while recognizing in all our activities the guiding hand of God.

Kate

—A Member of Al-Anon—

I've been in Al-Anon, a group for family members of alcoholics, since 1980. By then I'd been married to a recovering alcoholic for about ten years. When we were first married, I was twenty-seven years old and in love for the first time. He was my white knight in shining armor. Up until I met him, I felt empty and had no idea why. I didn't connect with men; I didn't really trust them. (I later found out I was sexually abused as a child.) Four months after we were married, I became a mother, because his ex-wife gave up their two children.

My husband was in AA, but I didn't know we were involved in an alcoholic marriage. It was like a merry-go-round: up when we were trusting and everything was good, and then straight down. Although my husband didn't drink anymore, he did gamble and couldn't hold a job. I loved and trusted as best I could, but amid all the "upping and downing" my trust level began to plummet. I'd married a diamond in the rough—a man of great intelligence, sensitivity, and creativity—and my mission, I decided, was to fix him, make him better, be his main support, and help him achieve his goals. Through him, I was going to fulfill my destiny.

When my parents moved from Wisconsin to Florida, we decided to move there as well. In Florida I worked as a recreational therapist, and my husband got a job as an alcoholic counselor at a treatment center fifty miles from our house. He would spend weekdays at the center and come home on weekends. After about two months, when I got a message at work that he wouldn't be returning for the weekend, I figured he was down because of the move. Well, he never showed up. I didn't even hear from him for two months.

His desertion was what brought me to Al-Anon. At first I

went to find out why he had left us and what could I do. I didn't realize that Al-Anon could help me with my own self-discovery, which before long was to change my life. In the beginning, I went to meetings five or six nights a week, because it was the only place I felt safe; it was my support, my reason for being. Then I almost died in a diabetic coma. While I was in the hospital, my husband called to say he'd run off to California with a younger woman and would come home to be with the children. At that point, with four months of meetings under my belt, I knew the spirit of our marriage had been broken.

Once back on my feet again, I attended a workshop called Music and Your Mind. That was my "aha" experience. Using music to go into the unconscious, I was able to see everything in a light that dissolved the veil between fantasy and reality, between myself and the world. Suddenly I realized I did not want to be married to my husband. The people at Al-Anon said I would know when to break off the marriage, and I trusted them—in fact, these meetings were my Higher Power, since at that point I could not connect with God. Sure enough, one afternoon I woke up from a nap knowing my marriage was finished, and I separated from my husband a few days later.

Although I had no self-esteem, I did believe what the program advocated and I also embraced the idea of a new way of life. The following years were complicated, but I got through them. Things began to ease up one night when I woke up to a voice saying, "Kate, why is it so easy for you to understand other people, but not yourself?" Hmm, I thought to myself, so I've been *teaching* what I need to *know!* With that discovery, I began to focus on self-understanding as a personal goal. I realized that I am a child of God and a gifted person. I saw that I was mirroring the people closest to me, and that all the admirable traits I'd seen in my ex-husband were what I wanted for myself. I realized how I had tried to make him fulfill my personal needs instead of developing myself. And I began to believe I *could* be as I wanted and do what I wanted.

Al-Anon has given me the strength and courage to take risks, to step beyond myself and try new things. Surprisingly, it has also awakened within me a deep compassion for the man who swooped me onto his steed and later abandoned me. More and more, as my truth has become my own, I've begun to empathize with his struggles rather than try to make him whole. I am happier today than ever before.

Compassion

*Now that my addiction is under control, I have
an opportunity to spread my love to others by making
amends to them for any wrongdoings.*

Making amends is a big step for many people, whether they have per-
petrated heinous crimes or less tangible transgressions. I never beat my
wife, for example, or abused my children, or committed a major offense,
although I did once misuse someone's credit card. Because the majority
of my offenses were emotional, I thought this would be an easy Step for
me. Wrong! Paying off the credit card debt was cushy compared to asking
my mother's forgiveness for resenting her after my father's death.

I then discovered that forgiving works both ways. After addressing
my own misdeeds, I could not sit back and wait for those who had
wronged me to make their amends, so I listed the offenses and active-
ly forgave each person for injuring me. Most of them I contacted by
phone, extending my forgiveness. Many of those I spoke with seized
the moment and made sincere restitution. A few were so moved that
they launched into their own recovery.

What catalyzes such acts of forgiveness is compassion—concern
for the well-being of others. We act compassionately when, recognizing
human failings, we reach out to others and ask their forgiveness, or
accept forgiveness from those who have injured us. In this way, we

acknowledge not only our common faults but the potential for change, which transcends them. Certainly, most of us feel compassion for victims of war, earthquakes, and other natural disasters; we give money, send food, and organize rallies on their behalf. But can we be just as compassionate toward a driver who has nearly plowed into us, or a waitress who gets our order wrong?

The Ninth Step is a direct challenge to the inherent nobility that slumbers within us. To buy a cup of coffee for someone who has just humiliated us is a truly compassionate gesture. But what about telling a friend that you've been sleeping with his wife, or informing your boss that you've been stealing office supplies? What constitutes an act of compassion usually depends on the greatest good for all concerned. Considering your friend's propensity for jealousy, it might be best to terminate the affair without saying a word, whereas a boss with high standards of honesty may demand a full accounting, even if it means losing your job.

Step Nine is Step Eight set into action. Reflection 27, "We Are All Open Books," explores the effects of being out of harmony with God's will. Reflection 28, "The Value of Firsthand Experience," explains why to actively search for our own truth instead of accepting that of others. Reflection 29, "Staying on Course," shows the importance of rectifying our misdeeds as soon as they occur.

REFLECTION 27

We Are All Open Books

Each of us is blessed with a moral barometer that alerts us to deviations from God's will for us and others. When the deviations are our own, even if we have followed the letter of God's law but defied its spirit, we will be promptly notified. Most often, the first signs of a violation appear in the physical body. Some form of dis-ease may set in—anything from a headache to an upset stomach to a strained muscle. If symptoms are ignored, the imbalance may develop into a full-blown illness with symbolic overtones. Hardening of the arteries, for instance, is sometimes interpreted as obstruction in the free flow of joy, and cancer as the will running wild. Or the dis-ease may impact on our mental processes, evoking confusion, anxiety, or fear.

When a person we meet has violated God's law, our moral barometer is apt to register in more subtle yet equally profound ways. Carl Jung once told the remarkable story of a woman who came to him for help. She confessed that out of jealousy toward a friend who was engaged to a wealthy landowner, she intentionally spooked her friend's horse while they were out riding. The horse reared and threw her friend to the ground, killing her. The woman used the mourning period to work her way into the affections of the landowner, whom she eventually married. However, she discovered that horses, even her favorite mount, would not let her ride them; that dogs and children ran from her; and that even her closest friends shied away. The shunning of this woman suggests that on some level we are open books to one another—that there are no secrets from God, humanity, or as is illustrated in this story, all of nature.

Whereas offenses make us undesirable, virtuous deeds have quite the opposite effect. They seem to open the floodgates to spirit that then pours through us, producing a certain glow. Others, sensing our light, are attracted to it. We all know people whose popularity stems not from their wealth or good looks, but from the deeds they perform, indicating that spirit broadcasts this information to others.

A friend of mine, for example, went for a job interview with a couple in a small Midwestern town. After reviewing his résumé and discussing salary, the couple took my friend for a walk through town to get to know him better. At one corner after another, they seemed to attract a variety of neighborhood dogs—a most unusual occurrence, according to the couple. My friend was hired that day, and some months later they confided that although they'd had no doubts about him, they figured if animals liked him that much he must be all right.

So it is that misdeeds carry their own penalty and, as William Shakespeare has reminded us, "virtue hath its own reward." Stated in other terms, every deviance from God's will imprints itself on the world, as does every act of compassion.

REFLECTION 28

The Value of Firsthand Experience

While compiling the list of injuries we have inflicted, we may begin to wonder about our chaotic journey through life and the meaning of it all. "Why," we might ask, "must I struggle in ignorance and cause so much harm to myself and others? Why did God arrange things this way?" The answer seems to lie in the biblical phrase "The Word was made flesh, and dwelt among us," suggesting that our souls are slivers of God. Our task is to use these divine sparks to perfect ourselves and all we touch, moving everything to its highest level, and thus back to God.

This we do through experience, our greatest and most devoted teacher. Closing ourselves off from life's hardships, a cocoonlike side effect of most addictions, is one way of denying God's plan for us and of keeping the Word disembodied. On the contrary, in delving into our human adventure—stumbling, falling, and crawling along to reach our goals—we transform with each act of love, forgiveness, and compassion not only ourselves but all of creation. To engage with life is to engage with God.

While immersing ourselves in life, we learn our own truths. If instead we nourish ourselves on the messages propounded in books, movies, music, and various media—in effect, on the gospel "according to others"—we end up living vicariously. The truths that transform us and fulfill our soul's mission are those derived from seeking out our own experiences: putting ourselves to the test, stepping into the fire, and letting it purify us. The Buddha so strongly advocated this path that he stated, "If you meet the Buddha on the road, kill him." In effect, he was advising his followers not to accept another's wisdom without first verifying it for themselves.

Mid-nineteenth–century author Henry David Thoreau offered similar advice. "Which student would have advanced the most," he asked, "the boy who had made his own jackknife from the ore which he had dug and smelted, reading as much as would be necessary for this, or the boy who had attended the lectures on metallurgy at the Institute in the meanwhile, and had received a Rodgers penknife from his father?" The answer is, the boy who made his own knife. Those of us who live our lives fully, and actively discover our own best path to travel, Thoreau assured us, nurture our soul's slow maturation through our often stressful existence. When we finally arrive at spiritual union, our experiences become growth rings, increasing as we evolve toward ultimate perfection.

Spiritual growth must be earned, often at great risk, which enhances its value. It is in wandering away from the purity and safety of spirit, and into frightening, dark regions that we gather this precious pearl.

REFLECTION 29

Staying on Course

You might think a driver foolish if, after realizing he'd taken a wrong turn, he traveled on for another hour before navigating his way back to his chosen route. Perhaps our greatest errors, too, come when we fail to quickly rectify our obvious "wrong turns." Without making amends, we may easily reverse much of our progress in recovery, if not end up all the way back at the starting point. In the process, we may lose our health, our friends, and our connection to spirit. Although energy is never wasted and no experience is for naught, the shortest distance between two recovery Steps is a straight line.

In a sense, each injury we cause yet fail to address is a side road that can lead us off our chosen path. Ignoring these injuries may work for a while, but eventually one of the "curves in the road" will pull us off track and have us driving around blind until we reverse our course and make amends. For greatest success, we need to rectify each injury we have incurred; otherwise, it will work on us at an unconscious level, weakening our resolve or tempting us to commit repeated transgressions.

A rule of the road is that we will never go astray if our actions are guided by God's commandment to love one another. In the Buddha's words, "Hatred does not cease by hatred at any time: hatred ceases by love—this is the eternal law." When we truly love others, be they friend or enemy, it becomes impossible to act wrongly and be pulled off our path. Similarly, it becomes impossible to disallow others the right to live freely, make mistakes, and *refuse* to atone for their wrongdoings. Even if we show up at the home of such an individual with our hand extended and they slam the door on us, we've done our part and need to let God do his.

Parents, especially, must remember to allow their children this freedom of choice. After all, how can they experience the trials of life and learn the way of spirit without charting a course of their own? In the end each of us, informed by spirit, must select for ourselves the options that best suit our evolution.

Sandra

—A Member of Workaholics Anonymous—

I am a workaholic. Before I came into Workaholics Anonymous (WA), I thought about work almost all the time. It was as much a mental addiction for me as drinking alcohol is a physical addiction for others. Although I was an at-home mom, I volunteered so often that I was on the phone constantly, telling my kids to "wait a minute" while I set up one program or another. Not only did I put off my kids and spouses, but I shelved my own interests; I was just too busy to take time for them. Basically, my addiction was to overcommitment: I only had time to keep up with tasks I'd committed to, and by the time those were finished I had already obligated myself to many more tasks. With this addiction, you rarely take time for recreation and enjoyment.

I've always worked two or three jobs at once, maybe because my self-esteem soars each time someone holds me in high regard. One of my recent jobs was with a do-gooder, not-for-profit organization—an arena filled with workaholics. When you're contributing to the greater good in this way, people think you're a better-than-average person, so you need to work harder and do more. And I had to do more than anyone else there. Still, my heart felt a little empty when I discovered this isn't what life is supposed to be like.

Ever since entering WA, I've remained aware of how the Steps apply to my addiction. Every morning, I try to turn it over to God through the first Three Steps: I say that I am powerless over my addiction, that I am a workaholic, and I ask God to give me guidance and relief from this obsession. Each night, I do a complete inventory of the day.

Soon after joining the program, I decided to go to law school. That was when I started listening to what I really wanted instead of being driven by what I'd already obligated myself to do, which was a big change for me. Since I'm a single mom now, being in school is an especially big deal. Although the legal profession is rife with workaholics, I'm conscious that I chose it for myself and don't have to be that kind of lawyer. My Twelve-Step work is helping me learn to say, "God will take care of me and give me what I need to do," which prevents me from getting plugged into an obsession. In the midst of all the studying, it also gives me a focal point for grappling with a basic tenet of WA: When you're not working, don't think about work. That's part of what I've been moving toward.

My life is a lot simpler and more effective than it was before WA. I get much more done, too, because I'm able to think about what I'm *doing* instead of listening to the constant chatter in my head about what I *ought* to be doing. Persistently approaching each day for itself has helped me clear away that mushrooming cloud and just be in the moment.

Persistence

*Just as I didn't acquire my addiction overnight,
it will take me time to recover from it, but I now believe
that my persistence will pay off.*

Like many of us, I usually think I'm right and see my actions as fair and high-minded, so when it came to Step Ten and I started to take a daily inventory, I was in for quite a surprise. Honestly recording my actions and attitudes on a daily basis punctured a huge hole in my self-satisfaction. I noted the effects of my quick temper, my chauvinistic attitudes, and a host of other offensive behaviors and traits I'd been unaware of. Although it may be tempting to overlook such indiscretions during the first or second week on this Step, the more we persist with our daily inventories, the more likely we are to either acknowledge our shortcomings and reform ourselves or fall out of recovery.

Taking a personal inventory need not be a negative experience. For one thing, we often discover as many positive deeds as negative ones, and each bit of progress deserves some form of congratulatory acknowledgment. For another, any time we feel depressed by our failings or hopeless about recovery, we can reach out for the warmth and camaraderie of our home group. Members talking openly about their lives, describing their challenges, even airing their dirty laundry humanizes our "ledger." Listening to them, we are no longer able to consider ourselves the black sheep of society. When called upon to talk, we can then open up and discuss our lives in a manner that we would have previously broached only after a few drinks. In response, newcomers quickly see that recovery is an intensely personal journey—that everyone has their own ways of fording streams, from plunging in knee-deep to dancing over slippery rocks. If some group members' approaches seem a bit strange, keep in mind the wisdom I was given early in my recovery: Instead of looking for differences, focus on similarities.

How we conduct a personal inventory can vary as much as the content we review. Whereas one person may list their feelings and actions on paper, another will record them in a mental file, or on index cards to be placed in a fliptop card file—with offenses up front, restitutions in back. What matters is not the approach we use but the continuity we bring to it. The more consistent we are in promptly admitting our mistakes and making amends, the more revelatory the experience will be, moving us ever closer to ongoing self-awareness.

Step Ten encourages us to work constantly toward improving ourselves. Reflection 30, "Cultivating Good Habits," shows how our conduct can either help or harm us on our spiritual journey. Reflection 31, "Think Sick, Be Sick," explores how spirit affects the mind and mind affects the body, and the importance of having all three vehicles in sync. Reflection 32, "The Value of Quiet Contemplation," points out the role of silence and solitude in the quest to connect with spirit.

REFLECTION 30

Cultivating Good Habits

Part of any thorough inventory is an evaluation of the habits around which our lives revolve. Habits, like the foods we eat or fluids we drink, are as good as the positive effects they promote. Therefore, in evaluating a habit, the first question to ask is this: Does it promote my physical, mental, emotional, and spiritual well-being?

The answer will depend on your individual makeup. For instance, engineers have an innate propensity for logic, order, and precision. They may find it beneficial to arise early and eat, sleep, even play at pre-determined times. Artists, on the other hand, tend to thrive on spontaneity, living from moment to moment and allowing passion to direct their activities. A supportive rhythm for an engineer would probably emphasize regularity, whereas for an artist it might be more intuitive.

Just as good habits help us achieve our goals, bad habits disrupt our natural orientation, destroying the tenor of daily activities and distracting us from our objectives. Worse, enforcing an unnatural rhythm can transform a bad habit into an addiction, causing us to deny our true self.

Typologists have arrived at four basic psychological orientations: thinking, feeling, intuiting, and sensing. A predominantly thinking type of person will be nurtured by mental stimuli more than, for instance, an intuitive type will be. The object is to abide by our innate propensities without overhabituating to an orientation, since doing so may deaden our natural responsiveness and curtail the development of our consciousness.

How do we tell a bad habit from a good one, or know when a bad habit has turned into an addiction? As before, we can analyze the habit's effects: Does it bring us closer to our higher self or take us further away? Does it enhance our relations with others or increase our self-absorption and aloofness? We can also contemplate whether or not our spiritual role model—such as Martin Luther King, Mother Theresa, Thomas Merton, the Dalai Lama, or Mahatma Gandhi—would advocate this course. The inquiry "What would Jesus do?" has become a guiding question for many people.

If it turns out that we are indulging in a bad habit or an addiction, we would do well to retrace Steps One through Three, admitting our powerlessness over it and asking God or our Higher Power to remove it. One of the finest habits we can cultivate is to constantly remind ourselves of spirit's inner presence. With practice, this awareness can become so ingrained in us that any time we are faced with an intractable habit, we will automatically raise our hearts in prayer.

REFLECTION 31

Think Sick, Be Sick

A critical component of any personal inventory is attitude, for this is often what determines the actions we so assiduously record. Our attitude, or the tenor of our thinking, is usually first felt in the body. This direct correlation between mind and body—a tenet underlying most complementary health practices, as well as the traditional medicine of the Far East—can be expressed in simple terms: To think "sick" is to be sick. Surely, a negative mental outlook fuels illness in much the same way an upbeat attitude promotes health. The body is simply the mind's obedient servant, responding to its subtle instructions as readily as it does to an outside stimulus, such as a head-on collision.

How, then, do we direct the mind to maximize our well-being? The answer is quite simple. Just as the body responds to the mind, the mind responds to spirit. By turning our will over to our Higher Power, we can open a conduit between spirit, mind, and body that leads to healthy living at all levels. So it is that in directing our hopes, aspirations, and talents toward God—through meditation, prayer, and constant awareness of spirit in our daily affairs—we place our health in God's capable hands.

One person who did just that was Christian Science founder Mary Baker Eddy, who later wrote: "There is no life, truth, intelligence, or substance in matter. All is infinite Mind and its infinite manifestations, for God is All in All." Eddy, a former invalid who had exhaustively applied medical cures, was healed only through her faith and her work with the mind. "Think well, be well" could have been her motto, and can certainly be ours.

The Value of Quiet Contemplation

The most effective mode for taking a personal inventory is quiet contemplation. It creates a space for spirit to enter and assist us in assessing our actions and attitudes, and in handling our retribution. The best strategy is to practice quiet contemplation during a peaceful time of day, perhaps an hour before your partner and children wake up in the morning, or after they've gone to bed at night. Initially, you may also want to hike or crochet alone on weekends to reinforce your connection to spirit.

In addition to setting the stage for inventory-taking, the practice of quiet contemplation fulfills the ongoing need for solitude and the experience of spiritual solace that we all have yet rarely respect. Companionship, although enjoyable and often supportive, pulls us out of ourselves, and today's accelerated pace of life tends to keep us there. Both our work settings and leisure time are cluttered by so much noise, electronic and human, that we can hardly hear ourselves think. We go from a blasting TV to a car radio or stereo to an office filled with electronic buzzing and human chatter. The world seems too much with us all—far more, perhaps, than we were designed for.

Jesus frequently escaped from the city, and from the camaraderie of his followers, to seek solitude in the hills, restoring his spiritual equilibrium through intense communion with God. We need not retreat to such isolated surroundings to feel the pulse of the divine presence within us; it may suffice to simply withdraw from the mainstream of human activity, turning off radios, TVs, computers, and telephones. "Be still," we are told, "and know that I am God." This stillness of solitude is at the core of an integrated spiritual life. Each time we delve deeply within ourselves to consummate a mystical union with spirit, we will undoubtedly emerge with a loving, grateful heart—which may be among our greatest spiritual discoveries.

Paradoxically, it is in silence that we hear God's "humming"—the symphony of the spheres, as some call it, or the ring of the universe—a background sound with swells and wakes that echo the roar of the ocean's surf. It is in silence that we perceive this cosmic whisper guiding, instructing, encouraging, and loving us. And it is in silence that we come to understand our relationship with all that is, from starry nightscapes to the earth's animals and vegetation. Cherish the silence as you would a great jewel, for from it comes the wisdom and love that resound in the essence of your being.

Jake

—A Member of Double Trouble in Recovery—

I'd been in AA for about two years when I got diagnosed with multiple personality disorder, or as the medical profession now calls it, dissociative identity disorder (DID). Actually, I knew something was wrong, because for a long time it felt like I was five different people. I finally went to see a therapist, and when he uncovered twenty *more* personalities I told him, "We're going backwards." I also knew things weren't right because I had trouble sharing my problems at the AA meetings—I got nothing but rejection from the group, and I felt isolated. I was sober, but crazy as a loon. I didn't know which of my personalities was talking and the group didn't understand what I was saying.

Then my sponsor told me about Double Trouble in Recovery—a program for recovering addicts with a medically diagnosed psychiatric disorder, most of whom are on prescription drugs. I had always felt myself surrounded by a protective shield so thick and heavy it could never be lifted. I was wrong. My first day in this program, it lifted. I stood up and talked about my problems as a multiple; and ever since, they haven't been able to shut me up. Sometimes I think I say too much, and sometimes I think it's not enough. Whatever it is, I don't really care. The point is that this is the only meeting in town where I can share my difficulties from the heart and get understanding.

At the other meetings, I was misinterpreted and always afraid of saying this or that. At Double Trouble meetings, I stopped trying to control the outcome. Sharing what's going on with me, I've found, helps me stay in the "now." Also, people there have shown me tools to help me deal with my condition. My sponsor, a therapist who has had experience with DID, told me, "Every single one of your personalities is going to do the Steps." That was mind-boggling to hear, but later it seemed to make sense and I saw I had a long road ahead of me.

I now go to meetings three times a week—it's my way of ending the day. It sets me up for going home and being relaxed enough to do journaling or Step work. Lately I've been dialoguing, which one of the people in the program with more personalities than me told me to try. I dialogue on paper. While imagining one of my personalities sitting across from me, I ask it, "What's going on?" and it tells me. I write down the words and respond. This way, I'm not denying the needs and desires of the personalities. (I've found that if I don't acknowledge them I end up paying for my oversight.)

Another reason I go to meetings so often is that I see other people there with psychiatric disorders. I don't know if they are able to comprehend what's going on with me when I share, but it doesn't matter; I'm comfortable there. Even if they don't understand me, they accept me for who I am. This gives me the security to say and do whatever I choose without having to fight it out with people like my parents, which has landed me in jail.

Before I joined this program, my thinking was all screwed up. My AA sponsor had told me to read "We Agnostics," a chapter in AA's Big Book. I'd start, but get thoroughly pissed off and throw the book against the wall. I shattered three books that way. Today, I'm reading "We Agnostics" without that kind of reaction. I can see I'm slowly but surely being restored to sanity. It's like that thought came to me from my Higher Power, and now every day I'm looking up and thanking it. For me, that's an awesome change.

Gratitude

I thank my Higher Power
each moment for another victory
over my addiction.

One of my first acts in recovery, before I entered AA, was to instinctively get down on my knees and pray for God's intercession. After years of contending with the cunning and powerful enemy of addiction, I somehow knew I needed the help of a Higher Power to overcome it. Fortunately, my religious upbringing and familiarity with prayer came to my aid. Yet I had no idea that prayer would become my ultimate recovery tool, and that expressing my gratitude through prayer would keep this avenue of communication open and active. So profound is the power of prayer that I now recommend this practice to everyone who seeks assistance.

We all know of people who acknowledge their addiction, enter a treatment center, and return to their habit after a relatively short-lived period of recovery. "Why can't they stay the course?" we ask ourselves. The greatest stumbling block to sustained recovery, it seems, is a person's unwillingness to establish and maintain contact with a Higher Power. Any time the main reason for getting clean is to keep a job, stay on a team, placate a judge, or contribute to a loved one's happiness, the person is still "managing" their addiction, and not surrendering it to God.

What I have learned from former "managers" I've worked with is that the best way to recover from an addiction is to recognize our power-lessness over it and then ask a Higher Power to remove it. In humbly thanking the Higher Power for its assistance, we go even further, completing the loop in the lifeline that links us to the source of wisdom within us.

It is important to note that the Twelve Steps embrace every religion's understanding of a Higher Power. Muslims pray to Allah five times a day. Followers of the Baha'i faith believe the earth is but one spiritually unified country, and humankind its citizens. As the Sufi poet Rumi wrote in *A Great Wagon,* "There are hundreds of ways to kneel and kiss the ground." And behind each of them, formalized or not, is the recognition of a Supreme Being whose guidance we are encouraged to summon at will. The method most frequently suggested is that of prayer.

I have often witnessed the profound power of prayer. When I first became sober, I prayed for my mother-in-law, who had evicted me from her house because I'd blamed her for my wife's alcoholism. Three weeks later, my mother-in-law broke her leg and required round-the-clock nursing care. One night I agreed to stay with her until my wife could take over. Before leaving home, I told our children to pray for their grandmother at 8:00 P.M. When I arrived at about 6:30 P.M., I talked to her about God, love, and forgiveness. By 8:00, we were hugging and asking each other's forgiveness. Although I divorced my wife a few months later and never saw my mother-in-law again, my children frequently regaled me with stories about how sweet she'd become in her old age.

One evening during our AA men's group, a well educated yet very drunk man wandered in and sat down. "The name's William," he muttered. "Whatcha got going here?" We talked about our problems with alcohol and solutions proposed by the Twelve Steps, and invited him to come to our next meeting. He returned, drunk again and wearing a stethoscope around his neck. William came to several more meetings in much the same condition; he didn't seem to be getting the message. Then one of our longtime members suggested we pray for him, which we proceeded to do. He showed up clean and sober at our next meeting and has been working in alcoholic treatment centers ever since. I later learned the reason for the stethoscope: before alcohol had taken over his life, William had been a well-respected pediatrician with a large practice.

Prayer is a vehicle not only for asking God to intercede in other people's lives but also for talking to our Higher Power about our *own* lives. We can discuss our problems; express our need for protection, direction, healing, or information; ask for help in difficult circumstances. And always we say thank you, whether or not we initially like what comes. Expressing our gratitude keeps us plugged in to the cosmic hot line that in reflective moments brings us counsel. Our thank-yous, uttered silently or out loud, open our hearts and teach us to trust that whatever is happening under the tutelage of our Higher Power is for the best. So it is that each offering of thanks enhances our conscious contact with God.

In Step Eleven, we improve on our connection with spirit by giving thanks. Reflection 33, "Reveling in the Presence of God," discusses how spirit imbues every moment of our lives. Reflection 34, "Gaining Knowledge of God's Will for Us," points out the value of doing God's will as we best see it. Reflection 35, "Faith versus Fear," defines fear and illustrates faith's capacity to overcome it.

Reveling in the Presence of God

A quick glance around us will reveal a natural world filled with miracle after miracle—everything from a field of brilliant red tulips to a towering majestic redwood to fiery yellow-and-orange skies at sunset. Albert Einstein once remarked that we can discover the meaning of everything by observing the natural world. Henry David Thoreau noted, "Nature is full of genius, full of the divinity; so that not a snowflake escapes its fashioning hand."

God's works, all wonders to behold, are clearly visible to us. However, the chaos of daily living can keep us so preoccupied that we do not see them. Not noticing the works of God in nature, we tend to forget that we, too, are under divine influence every hour of every day. That's not to say we are puppets pulled by strings, but rather that spirit lives, moves, and has its being in the human soul. Blessed with free will, we can either accept or reject its constant flow of power and wisdom.

Imagine a gentle spring rain. We can collect it in barrels to later quench the thirst of plants and flowers. We might even celebrate the coming rebirth of nature's glory by bathing in its soft waters. Or we can stay indoors and complain that the downpour has spoiled our after-noon plans, or our child's baseball practice. Given the opportunity to accept or reject God's love, in whatever form it happens to appear, the degree to which we allow it to enter our lives marks the difference it will make in our recovery.

How do we come to accept divine love? Often, through our higher consciousness—a faculty that evolves over many lifetimes of suffering or, as in the apostle Paul's illumination on the road to Damascus, in a flash of sudden, unquestionable awareness. Both methods give way to a crystal-clear perception of God's presence in the world. If we are too engrossed in life's complexities to receive information from our higher consciousness, we can always look around us to see how others are availing themselves of this innate resource. From a family member, we may observe that God's love can transform sickness into health and harmony. From a friend or neighbor, we may learn that God's love can instantly change sadness into joy, and even mend a broken heart. "Here," we may conclude, "is all the help I need to live a happy and successful life."

Having discovered God's love in the world and welcomed it into our lives, we may be inspired to turn to it in pleasant times as well as in times of hardship. Toward this end, let us spontaneously express gratitude for the many gifts of spirit, and be reverently thankful for the parts they play in transforming our lives. As we sit down to dinner, let us thank the farmers who grew the food we are about to eat, the entire food chain that brought nourishment to our plate, and God for providing the spark of life that animates all creation. The secret to a successful, vibrant existence is to be constantly aware of and ever grateful for the pervasive power of spirit in our midst.

REFLECTION 34

Gaining Knowledge of God's Will for Us

How do we uncover God's plan for us? Such a task ought to be simple, since it is in our best interest to access this information, yet it is far from easy. It requires us to quiet our incessant mind chatter, examine our personal desires, and learn to distinguish God's will from our own projections. In effect, gaining knowledge of God's will is a form of initiation requiring us to purify ourselves and retreat into silence. At such times, we may be led along strange paths, each one representing an unresolved issue that must be swept away before our true mission can be revealed.

A radical example of this initiation comes from the Kogi tribe of Colombia, who place prospective shamans, usually children, in a cave for nine years. Throughout their subterranean sojourn, their provisions are furnished but they are allowed no human contact. Living in near total darkness, they become attuned to the spirit world and begin to communicate intimately with A-Luna, the "mind inside nature." This dialogue prepares them to interpret the will of spirit for their tribe.

It is the sine qua non of existence to understand God's will for us. In prayer, we ask for it; in meditation, we receive it. Then we strike out boldly, courageously, and faithfully for the pathways these inner promptings reveal, aware that there are no guarantees of an immediately successful outcome. The paths can lead to deep fulfillment or they can wander off into the desert of illusion; they can elicit crowd applause or the silence of the forest. Rather than judge the results too quickly, we must continually repeat the prayer of the pilgrim: "Whatever, Lord, wherever—let thy spirit lead me."

When we pray for the strength to fulfill God's will, as spiritual leaders throughout history have done under the worst possible conditions, we need to accept that the path ahead lies shrouded in mystery. Knowing, too, that the adventure is infinitely worthwhile, we place our faith in divine intelligence and follow its dictates no matter where they may lead us.

REFLECTION 35

Faith versus Fear

Fear is a lack of faith in the divine order. When we doubt our understanding of God's will for us, or that God *has* a rewarding plan for us, we fall prey to nameless dreads, a thousand fears—in short, a torturous existence. At every turn in life, we confront haunting questions: Can I trust in my partner's loyalty, my children's honesty, my company's fairness, my president's wisdom, or will they betray me? Certainly, if we have placed our faith in people, we may be disappointed; but when we root our faith in the divine order, we know that all outcomes, whatever they may be, are the result of an intelligence greater than our own.

Fear is also will based. We fear that a prize we want may not come our way, and if it eludes us we blame the universe for letting us down. Or we fear germs and wash our hands a hundred times a day, or we fear the loss of love, the onset of old age, or the expropriation of basic necessities—all the while investing great faith in the power of our will. When we opt for God's will over our own, on the other hand, we notice the significant spiritual growth that can come from falling ill, losing a loved one, being homeless for a while, or other trials that would test the faith of Job.

Whereas fear comes in a thousand varieties, there is only one form of faith: absolute. How do we acquire such faith? How do we muster enough of it to venture into the unknown—to "walk on water" when all our senses tell us it cannot be done? For some, faith is born of pure devotion, in this lifetime or those past. For most, it comes with trading in the bottle, the drug, or the obsession, for the path of sobriety. Doubts and fears are to faith like a drink is to a recovering alcoholic; there are no half-measures. You place your faith fully in the divine plan. Hence the path of sobriety calls for determination, singleness of purpose, and an unshakable belief that the best possible outcome will prevail.

Many people regard this conviction of faith as their greatest accomplishment. For some, it comes early in life; for others, it emerges in midlife or later, often in response to a great trial; for still others, it announces itself on their deathbed, when a deep belief in the soul's continuation suddenly surfaces, obliterating their fear of annihilation. Seekers of faith, *whenever* they turn to spirit, are richly and rapidly rewarded. As it is written in the Bible, "Ask, and it shall be given you … knock, and [the door] shall be opened."

Robby

—A Member of Nicotine Anonymous—

I was addicted to cigarettes for nearly forty years before joining Nicotine Anonymous (NA). For me, smoking was very complicated. I'd smoke anywhere, even in the shower. I would wake up in the morning, smoke two cigarettes before getting out of bed, and say, "To hell with it." I couldn't help myself. I was as defeated as an alcoholic who doesn't bother to get up, take a shower, and put on some clothes. I couldn't even make an effort to stop smoking. The habit had completely overtaken me.

I did quit smoking—twice. The first time lasted a week. I was eighteen years old and taking a college physical-education course that had me feeling like a military recruit in basic training. Sweating the nicotine out of my pores broke the physical addiction. Then I got so fit I could run a mile and follow it up with a nonfiltered cigarette without breaking my stamina. Being so healthy that I could smoke was my big coup. The second time I quit by chewing a substitute gum, but I chewed so much of it that I turned brown from all the nicotine. My doctor took me off the gum, and I got raging mad at him and went back to smoking. Repressed anger, it turned out, was a big part of my cigarette habit.

With nicotine, after a momentary high you feel anger, and then you feel guilty and get sad about it—glad, mad, sad. It's like going on a big drunk and having tons of remorse afterward. My feelings, my thinking, everything was mixed up with anger. Finally, I stopped smoking cold turkey for a week, but I knew I still needed help. The night I set off for my first NA meeting, I ended up driving around the block three times before heading over there. After the first thirty days, I was past the physical addiction to nicotine. Over the next thirty days, I dealt with the psychological addiction. That left the emotional addiction.

It felt unbelievably good to be physically and psychologically free of nicotine. But I soon developed an eating disorder.

So, a year after I stopped smoking, I entered a program to help me deal with my addiction to eating. At this point, I was getting my life together and had enrolled in a master's degree program in business administration. But the tuition drove me so deeply into debt that I ended up in Debtor's Anonymous as well. Here I was in business school and crippled with liabilities! DA helped me afford to continue the MBA program.

People call me a Twelve-Step Wonder Boy. With the nicotine, eating, and debting addictions, in addition to subsequent alcohol and drug addictions as well as being the adult child of an alcoholic and being codependent as hell, I've been in more programs than anyone I know. The good news is, they've all worked.

I stopped drinking and using drugs twenty-two years ago. Before that, people were telling me, "Robby, if you don't surrender to a Higher Power, you're not going to make it." Those words were ringing in my ears when I met a spiritual type of guy at a meeting and right away wanted to be like him. He assigned me to a tough sponsor who hammered the Twelve Steps into me. Four years later I was sober. Whereas before I couldn't pass a bar without stepping inside, I could now go anywhere in the world and not drink.

So here I am, fully sober. I've been promoted to a position that will bring me upwards of $80,000 a year. Thanks to the prompting of my Higher Power, I got baptized, converted to Catholicism, and joined the Knights of Columbus. One reason my life has turned around is that I haven't stopped reciting the Smoker's Prayer I learned at NA. It gives me ongoing opportunities to make continuous conscious contact—the three Cs—with my Higher Power. The thing to remember is, you're going to either make that contact or continue with your addiction.

I now believe that God gives us addictions so we can move consciously closer to him by overcoming them. But it is the people in the programs who provide the road map that leads us home. As one sponsor put it, "I sought my God, and my God I could not see. I sought my soul, and my soul eluded me. I sought my fellows, and I found all three."

Service

*Since I love myself
more than ever, I offer
God's love to each and to all.*

One morning while driving home on a four-lane highway, I noticed the car in front of me weaving from one lane to the next. As it went up and over a hill, I prayed for the driver. When I reached the crest of the hill, I saw that he had run his car off the road and impaled it on a large rock. The man was leaning against the car in a daze. I pulled over and walked up to him. Although drunk, he appeared free of injuries. I flagged his car and then drove him to his home, all the while talking about AA and how he'd bolstered my recovery. Did this man follow my advice and attend meetings? I have no idea, but I do know that God had placed him on my path and I'd done what I could for him.

Another time, I picked up a hitchhiker in New Jersey who had been drinking heavily. I took him to his home and then to a recovery group meeting, where I found him a sponsor. Three months later, I received a card with his signature and a brief message: "Thanks, buddy. Easy does it."

Helping another addict is always a privilege. Not only does it strengthen my resolve to stay sober, but it offers promise to the other person and, ultimately, to humanity. That's how the magic works. As

Bill W. and Dr. Bob, founders of Alcoholics Anonymous, discovered in 1935, and Jesus proposed more than two thousand years before, there is transformative power inherent in serving others—in this case, sharing one's knowledge, love, and sobriety with those in need. Certainly, since 1935 Alcoholics Anonymous has not only grown exponentially but also spawned countless Twelve-Step programs throughout the world, as we saw earlier.

Helping others can also lead to a spiritual awakening. Some people experience a sudden opening, whereas others transform more slowly—a little bit with each meeting they attend and each act of service they perform, until they feel a connection to the grand chain of being that is God. So it is that the Golden Rule, "Do unto others as you would have them do unto you," is no preachy edict, but rather life's secret dynamic. Dedicating ourselves to the recovery of others opens us to our own oneness with spirit.

Joseph Campbell, a mythologist who inspired countless storytellers from film producer George Lucas to poet Robert Bly, discovered a pattern underlying all great myths and fairy tales, which he called the "hero's journey." The supreme test of the hero is his willingness to share his newfound wisdom and knowledge with others having the same affliction as him—and with that comes his transformation. Such sharing, said Campbell, helps heal the wounded land of their forefathers. Without a doubt, every recovering addict is a hero who has faced tribulations tantamount to those of Hercules. And for us the final trial, the sharing of wisdom, assists in not only finding the self but honoring it by moving well beyond thoughts of self-preservation.

Step Twelve, which represents a return to the world after our spiritual resurgence, helps spread God's love to others. Reflection 36, "Love Is Giving to Others," reminds us that giving freely of the gifts we have received begins a chain of reciprocity that can transform even the harshest landscape. Reflection 37, "Two Ways to Receive More Love," reveals the twin secrets to experiencing an amplified flow of love.

REFLECTION 36

Love Is Giving to Others

When someone in distress needs assistance, how do most people respond? They tend to offer a few encouraging words or a small financial donation, and then quickly return to their everyday lives, with rarely a thought about the afflicted person. However, when an emergency arises, such as an accident or a natural disaster, most people respond with great urgency to rescue and sustain the victim, providing first aid, food, clothing, and shelter.

Why does it take a major calamity to draw the best out of people? Because we seem to have become emotionally numb—desensitized by the complexity and demands of contemporary life. In fact, according to several social analysts, people today are more driven by self-interest than any past generation. It takes a personal or public crisis to shatter our hard, crablike shells and awaken our sleeping hearts. Many Westerners, in particular, endorse rugged individualism to such an extreme that we expect people to either make it on their own or suffer as a result of their "fragility." If difficulties mount and the odds against survival suddenly soar, we shrug and declare, "So be it."

A man at a meeting once told of his childhood friend Frank, whose father lost his job as a civilian electrician at an East Coast naval shipyard. Their longtime next-door neighbor, a successful private contractor, considered employing Frank's father to fill a position but, as he put it, he didn't want to "get involved." Turning a cold shoulder to a friend in need, the contractor hired less qualified help and, a few years later, died of a heart attack in his early fifties.

How can we transmute today's arid emotional climate? Perhaps the solution lies in releasing the love locked in our hearts like a captive bird that yearns to fly. After all, it was former president Woodrow Wilson's love for his wife that transformed him into a champion of world peace. Similarly, movie star Arnold Schwarzenegger says that marriage and fatherhood transformed him from a loner into a community-minded person.

To be touched by love is to be forever changed. I will always remember the taxi driver who, when I mentioned I was about to present an advertising proposal, said she would pray for me, and the kind man who paid for a hotel room for a Marine and his wife on the eve of the young man's departure for World War II.

Jesus showed us the way of the heart by lavishing God's love on all who would receive it. Mother Teresa, Martin Luther King, and others continued the tradition, turning hundreds of isolated and lonely wanderers into spiritually alive bearers of kindness and assistance. If a single act of love can generate ripples of caring that radiate throughout the universe, imagine what an ongoing offering of love can do. This outpouring from the heart, portrayed so vividly in the biblical parable of the Good Samaritan, is a way of endlessly praising God.

The creation of a more loving world begins with each of us and the strides we take as we walk through Step Twelve. Do we boycott liquor stores and lobby to outlaw drive-up windows? Do we storm into casinos and preach to the croupiers? Hardly, for we know firsthand that the best way to spread hope for recovery is through example rather than rhetoric. When called upon, we feel privileged to answer an addict's questions, or to speak at a gathering, always protecting our precious anonymity. We know personally that it takes only a caring word, a kind gesture, and an open heart to summon a person's innate faith in the light at the end of the tunnel of remorse, despair, defeat, and degradation. Therefore, when confronted with the darkness of another's addiction, we simply and lovingly hold out our candle of recovery.

Two Ways to Receive More Love

It has been said that love is the driving force of creation, drawing together everything from molecules to stars in order to compose larger, more inclusive life forms. It is also the motivating factor behind all human endeavors, whether we work hard to provide for our children, seek success to win admiration, or strive to perform good deeds for their own sake. To block or deny the flow of love, or render it impotent, perpetrates the worst possible crime against ourselves and others, because a person who feels deprived of love experiences no reason for being. What we must remember is that whereas human love can be fickle, God's love, shared equally by all living beings, is ever present to sustain us and give purpose to our lives.

How can we draw more fully from this inexhaustible natural resource? The most direct way is by clearing the conduit between ourselves and God. This we do by cleaning out the sludge of anger, blame, and guilt, and by making our amends to others. To increase the flow of God's love, we constantly communicate with spirit through prayer and meditation, and as the bumper sticker urges us, practice Random Acts of Kindness.

Another way to receive more love is by directing our generosity toward the welfare of those less fortunate—people who are physically sick, mentally ill, poor, homeless, or addicted. This form of giving, to be maximally beneficial, requires more than a dollar handout to a homeless person or two more cans of soup to the Christmas food drive for the poor. It asks us to share our dedication, imagination, and creativity—God's gifts to us. Why? Because our offering will then find its way back to God. As Jesus said, "Inasmuch as ye have done it unto one of the least of these my brethren, ye have done it unto me."

TV star Dennis Weaver one day saw the massive amount of edible food thrown out by employees of a large grocery store in Los Angeles. After he talked with the owners, they were glad to give him the food, which he then personally distributed to the poor. Within months, a fleet of volunteers was picking up food from hundreds of stores and distributing it by truck throughout the city. This model of generosity soon spread to other cities and developed into a major charitable movement, much to Weaver's delight, as well as that of the store owners. When we assist others, divine love flows into our lives as surely as earth's gravitational field attracts falling objects, as any charitable person will confirm.

On a grander scale, plastic surgeons have been flying from the United States to Bolivia and Uganda to operate on children with birth defects, eventually bringing life back into the eyes of youngsters who were previously ostracized. While the world applauds the surgeons' heroic work, we need to remember that in God's eyes one kind word expressed with love and concern yields effects equivalent to those of any grand humanitarian gesture. In Mother Teresa's words, "We do no great things, only small things with great love."

We were meant to share what we have been given, and to reap enormous benefits as a result. As recovering addicts, we derive great strength from offering to another seeker of sobriety the wisdom our group has given us. In giving, we receive—a principle as profound as it is simple.

Continuing On in Recovery

Just as everyone who walks into a recovery group meeting does not walk out sober for life, neither do the Twelve Steps guarantee recovery. With sufficient commitment, however, sobriety is a realistic outcome for every one of us. In fact, it is almost impossible to follow the Steps for a sustained period of time without experiencing a remarkable transformation.

For this reason, we walk the Twelve Steps again and again, incorporating them ever more vigorously into our lives. Each time we complete Step Twelve, with our addiction farther behind us, we take it upon ourselves to again tread the path of self-discovery, finding ever deeper tap roots grounded in self-acceptance, visions of ourselves as loving human beings, and a strong desire to move forward in life.

To keep our lives as manageable as possible during this time, we also cultivate a harmonious lifestyle that weaves together the diverse facets of our existence. I start every day, for example, by thanking God in advance for protecting me against my addiction to alcohol, which sets in motion a safeguard mechanism. Whenever Jesus was to face a trial, he would pray beforehand; he'd pray, then his desires would become manifest in reality. Similarly, it has been said that science is based not on cause creating effect, but on effect creating the cause. In other words, envision the outcome and the means to achieve it will present themselves.

It is also important to take proper care of ourselves as each day unfolds, ensuring that we get enough rest, healthy nourishment, exercise, and time to connect with our Higher Power. Community is another vital factor. Maintaining relationships with a sponsor and the people in our Twelve-Step meetings reminds us that we are not alone and that our problems are not unique. While overly absorbed in our own dramas and obsessions, "passing the word" on to another person, even in a small way, can greatly expand our horizons.

Through creativity, we tap into the hidden recesses of our mind and spirit. Any creative activity that encourages us to express our feelings directly, rather than projecting them onto outside targets, is invaluable to our recovery. Honest communication with our sponsor is equally beneficial for preventing misunderstandings and emotional outbursts. While interacting with *anyone,* we would do well to not only listen to what they are saying but also "read" their body language. Taking an inventory of our personal relationships is an excellent prelude to clearing emotional baggage and strengthening our connection to others.

A day in which we rest, eat well, connect with friends and family, work, pray, exercise, and flex our creative muscles generally feels more rewarding than one in which we focus exclusively on one or two of these areas. To keep the energy flowing, we balance the day's activities. For instance, if we tend to overreact, we might follow a vigorous workout with quiet time rather than a business meeting.

Although we all have the capacity for conscious, happy living, our addictions have subverted our best intentions. While continuing on in recovery, we face each of these challenges head-on and clear away our demons, which allows our true strengths and abilities to finally surface. With that, we shift from being unwilling victims in life to willing participants in an existence viewed as part of a greater plan.

THE MYTH OF "LOST" OPPORTUNITIES

During recovery, it is best to stay in the present moment as much as possible. Of course, there will be days when we regret past mistakes, chide ourselves for wrong turns in the road, long for what could have been if our lives had been different. Eventually, however, we come to see that such "lost" opportunities, wasted time, and unfulfilled passions were actually to our soul's benefit, as the following Persian fairy tale suggests:

> There were once three princes of Serendip. Two of
> the princes battled with their neighbors to acquire huge
> tracts of land, fleets of ships, and war booty. The third

prince was content with his possessions and even counseled his brothers against colonizing the neighboring states.

One day, his brothers decided to lead the country into war. The peaceful prince urged against it but was quickly overruled. Serendip began to prepare feverishly for this campaign, with war drums beating night and day. Finally, preparations were complete and the country's young men were poised for battle.

Suddenly, a tremendous windstorm arose, lashing the earth with rain and hail for three days. When the storm subsided, the damage to the assembled ships was colossal—wreckage strewed the harbor. What's more, buildings lay toppled in pools of water and the contents of the granary, completely destroyed, sprawled in all directions.

Dispirited, the people of Serendip feared famine and trembled at the thought of an invasion. Recognizing their weakened state, the three princes reassembled their counsel and decided to forgo the planned conquest, whereupon the people returned to their daily pursuits of planting, plowing, and gathering what had been sown.

"Look at the opportunity we have lost—to grow, become powerful, and acquire great wealth!" cried the two defeated princes. The third prince turned to the sacred writings of the people and quieted his brothers with these words: "Greater is he who conquers self than one who conquers a city."

From this mid-eighteenth–century fairy tale came the word *serendipity,* naming the human faculty for finding value in unsought circumstances.

Faith, like serendipity, wells up within us, assuring us that God's will is in our highest, best interest, and that what may appear as lost opportunities are actually blessings in disguise. Even when we believe that a wish has been denied us, if we keep ourselves open to God's will a new opportunity will soon appear to redirect our energies toward growth and a brighter future.

People confronted with lost opportunities have made remarkable discoveries that might not otherwise have come to light. Energy runs high, vigilance increases, and patience, as the adage goes, brings its own rewards. Approaching this somewhat altered state, a young man reported to his wise mentor that he had been fired from his job. The mentor took out a bottle of wine, poured two glasses, and offered a toast, saying, "At least you weren't promoted. Now all your opportunities are *before* you."

During times of defeat, our job is to remain steadfast to our belief in a divine plan. In doing so, we may begin to perceive our situation as a sailor views a shifting wind, certain that it is time to adjust the sails, change course, and ply onward. Potters will sometimes go further, *intentionally* breaking a vessel they have been shaping—an act that realigns their focus and often results in the creation of a superior pot.

Vigilance is advised. When an opportunity first knocks, listen; when it knocks again, go to the door; at the third knock, open the door and bid it to enter. If you are listening carefully, you are likely to hear spirit inviting you to leave your door open to its surprises.

HOW TO ACHIEVE PEACE

Think about the peace that transcends all understanding, the tranquillity that pervades the human heart when we feel God's presence stirring within us. Peace is at once a calming of the senses and a stilling of the turbulent emotions that course through us on any given day.

What is the nature of this magic that subdues our agitated mind and rebellious feelings? The essence of peace is oneness with ourselves, with the world around us, and with God's will for us. Its call is for surrender. We feel peace when we have surrendered our will to our highest, best interest.

There are many ways to achieve peace. One is by deliberately calming the pace of our hectic lives. Another is by cultivating "bifocal" consciousness, directed outward as we exhale and inward as we inhale—a practice that quiets and centers the mind while deflecting life's distractions. Peace is also amenable to meditation and to visualization. In times of stress or temptation, visualizing a symbol of spirit, such as an angel or a saint or a virtuous person, can undercut the fears that drive our personal demons. Some people achieve excellent results from simply visualizing themselves in a tranquil setting.

Whatever method you choose, continue to practice peace. As you do, you are sure to realize that the soul—the eternal self—remains intact no matter what; that it is anchored securely to the permanence of God; and that when called upon, it will deal effectively with any upset. With continued recovery, revisit your eternal self as often as possible. There your whole being may throb with the awareness that "this, too, shall pass," dissolving into vapor by the flame of your eternal self.

LIVING THE SPIRITUAL LIFE

Once you have begun your journey into recovery and have familiarized yourself with the Twelve Steps, these suggestions may help you remain on the spiritual path as you move forward in your life:

1. Handle with respect and care the many gifts of spirit you embody, and use them with discretion. The more honored the gift, the more potent its effects.

2. In matters of money, be as generous as possible, and realize that what you give comes back to you ten-fold.

3. Release your anger and animosity toward others. Hatred poisons the soul and creates sickness and disharmony. Love others and you will feel God's love.

4. Rather than relying on the mind's understanding or the availability of material comforts, both of which may crumble in the first storm, place your faith in the still, small voice within you. Whatever difficulties you face, let your inner voice be your guiding star.

5. In your darkest moments, pause and reflect on the beauty around you. Take joyful respite in the wonders of nature, and seek peace in spirit's handiwork.

6. If given a choice between one path or another, follow the more rewarding one, even if it is the most difficult. Challenges are the soul's workouts.

7. Praise and thank your spiritual guides—your ever-present yet unseen companions who love you dearly.

8. When in doubt, pray for divine guidance. It will always be given.

9. Seek the presence of spirit in all you do, for existence holds no nobler purpose.

APPENDIX A

Self-Tests for Compulsive Behaviors

How can we tell if we are addicted and in need of assistance? Or for those of us already in a recovery group, how can we find out if we are ensnared in a more deeply buried, core addiction? In short, how do we know if our soul is seeking to awaken?

Such knowledge is not easily acquired. One reason it eludes us is that we live in an addicted culture where many people enjoy cocktails with dinner each night, an occasional joint to unwind, an evening at the casino from time to time, or visits to a bakery while feeling unloved. In a world where social amenities and pleasurable pastimes verge on the obsessive, it is difficult to know when a behavior has gotten the best of us. Then, too, we are creatures of denial, caught up in grand illusions of ourselves. Looking in a mirror, we are apt to say, "Not *me*. I'm no addict. I can stop any time I *want* to." Our illusions are sometimes pitiful as well, such as when we tell ourselves, "My life is a total mess. The only way out of this is *down*."

With true self-understanding so hidden from view, a good way to find out if we are in need of recovery is to embark on an archaeological dig. In we go, through our highly cultivated plots or our mud slides of denial, in search of our soul. In lieu of a pickax, we can use a self-test— a self-excavating tool par excellence. I know, because that is what worked for me forty years ago. An AA "Who Me?" quiz, which I seriously flunked, is what finally catapulted me to awakening and freedom.

To help you on your quest for self-knowledge, the following pages contain twelve self-tests, one for each addiction referred to in this book. Take whichever self-tests seem appropriate, making sure to "dig" in a quiet, private place. The digs may turn up slag or pure ore, sand or gold nuggets, in either case giving you valuable information about yourself. Also consider giving a self-test to a loved one. Three or more "yes" responses to any quiz signals a need for action, in which case you or your loved one may want to contact the corresponding support group listed in Appendix B.

A Self-Test for Compulsive Drinking

	YES	NO
1. If given a choice, do you prefer to drink alone?	[ ]	[ ]
2. Do you become physically or verbally abusive after a few drinks?	[ ]	[ ]
3. Do you believe that alcohol covers up your "inadequacies"?	[ ]	[ ]
4. Does excessive drinking diminish or erode your moral standards?	[ ]	[ ]
5. Is drinking becoming an ever increasing problem in all areas of your life?	[ ]	[ ]
6. Did either of your parents have a drinking problem?	[ ]	[ ]
7. Have you ever been arrested for driving while intoxicated?	[ ]	[ ]
8. When you look in a mirror, do you see the effects of your drinking?	[ ]	[ ]
9. Do you hide empty bottles of booze?	[ ]	[ ]
10. Have you ever stopped drinking only to start again?	[ ]	[ ]

A Self-Test for the Compulsive Use of Cocaine

	YES	NO
1. Have your experiences under the influence of cocaine stopped being fun?	[ ]	[ ]
2. Are you having serious financial problems?	[ ]	[ ]
3. Do you ever feel that you are in a pit so deep there is no way out?	[ ]	[ ]
4. Have you ever lied about your use of cocaine?	[ ]	[ ]
5. Do you sometimes use on your own?	[ ]	[ ]
6. Were you ever jailed, hospitalized, or in rehab for cocaine use?	[ ]	[ ]
7. Have you ever felt defensive, guilty, or ashamed about your using?	[ ]	[ ]
8. Are you having health problems?	[ ]	[ ]
9. Would you quit using if you could?	[ ]	[ ]
10. Have you ever contemplated suicide?	[ ]	[ ]

A Self-Test for Compulsive Overeating

	YES	NO
1. Do you like to eat alone, with no one watching how much you consume?	[ ]	[ ]
2. Does your partner know what you eat when you are alone?	[ ]	[ ]
3. Do you routinely combine eating with reading, or watching TV?	[ ]	[ ]
4. Do you have a secret "stash" of unhealthy foods that you crave?	[ ]	[ ]
5. Do you eat when you feel scared, frustrated, disappointed, or unloved?	[ ]	[ ]
6. Do you gorge yourself at night to relax from a stressful day?	[ ]	[ ]
7. Do you believe you will be able to lose some or all of your excess weight as soon as you set your mind to it?	[ ]	[ ]
8. Have you modified your wardrobe to disguise your added pounds?	[ ]	[ ]
9. Has overeating caused you to become self-conscious about your appearance?	[ ]	[ ]
10. Has a physician ever advised you to lose weight?	[ ]	[ ]

A Self-Test for Compulsive Sex and Love

	YES	NO
1. Is sex your primary link to other people, or to yourself?	[ ]	[ ]
2. Do you find that you need multiple sexual relationships to get physical and emotional satisfaction?	[ ]	[ ]
3. Have you ever had sex with someone you didn't really care for?	[ ]	[ ]
4. Has your sexual history caused you to become a "serial liar"?	[ ]	[ ]
5. Is shame a dominant emotion in your life?	[ ]	[ ]
6. Do you use sex to avoid dealing with problems?	[ ]	[ ]
7. Have you ever felt your life is out of control because of your sexual needs?	[ ]	[ ]
8. Do you sometimes want to let others in on this hidden part of yourself?	[ ]	[ ]
9. Is masturbation your secret ally?	[ ]	[ ]
10. Would you change your sexual behavior if you could?	[ ]	[ ]

A Self-Test for Compulsive Gambling

	YES	NO
1. Once you start gambling, is it very difficult to stop?	[ ]	[ ]
2. Do you get high from gambling?	[ ]	[ ]
3. Do thoughts of a nearby casino evoke a powerful urge to "try your luck"?	[ ]	[ ]
4. Have you ever lied about the extent of your gambling losses?	[ ]	[ ]
5. Have you promised your partner you'll never gamble again?	[ ]	[ ]
6. Do you spend much time thinking about gambling?	[ ]	[ ]
7. Have you ever borrowed money secretly to place a bet?	[ ]	[ ]
8. Do you feel guilt and shame over your inability to contain your gambling impulses?	[ ]	[ ]
9. Do you envy people who are able to maintain control over their gambling?	[ ]	[ ]
10. Would your life be better if you quit gambling?	[ ]	[ ]

A Self-Test for the Compulsive Use of Narcotics

	YES	NO
1. Do you use drugs to escape from problems?	[ ]	[ ]
2. Do you plan your life around drug use?	[ ]	[ ]
3. Do you find that your choice of friends is determined by your use of narcotics?	[ ]	[ ]
4. Have you ever not known what drug you were taking, or what its effect on you might be?	[ ]	[ ]
5. Do you feel remorseful about the way you sometimes act while using?	[ ]	[ ]
6. Did you ever steal in relation to your drug use?	[ ]	[ ]
7. Does your partner complain that your drug use is damaging your relationship?	[ ]	[ ]
8. Do you feel more and more desperate about your life?	[ ]	[ ]
9. Is it difficult to imagine a life without drugs?	[ ]	[ ]
10. Have you ever tried to quit using drugs?	[ ]	[ ]

A Self-Test for Compulsive Spending

	YES	NO
1. Is your spending a way to escape from problems?	[ ]	[ ]
2. Do you sometimes feel out of control when it comes to money?	[ ]	[ ]
3. Do you feel euphoric during or after a successful shopping expedition?	[ ]	[ ]
4. Do you stay awake at night wondering how to make ends meet financially?	[ ]	[ ]
5. Do you have significant credit card indebtedness?	[ ]	[ ]
6. Does your partner know the true extent of your financial liability?	[ ]	[ ]
7. Would you like to borrow money to eliminate all your debts?	[ ]	[ ]
8. Do you spend money on recreation instead of satisfying your financial commitments?	[ ]	[ ]
9. Do you sometimes justify an expenditure by telling yourself you will "work it out" later?	[ ]	[ ]
10. Have you ever curbed your splurging only to resume the pattern of spending beyond your means?	[ ]	[ ]

A Self-Test for Compulsive Codependency

	YES	NO
1. Do you often feel angry, scared, lonely, or victimized?	[ ]	[ ]
2. Do you tend to hide your true emotions?	[ ]	[ ]
3. Do you let other people make decisions for you?	[ ]	[ ]
4. Do you need to get high to have fun?	[ ]	[ ]
5. Is it difficult to accept criticism or praise?	[ ]	[ ]
6. Do you sometimes use rage to get your way?	[ ]	[ ]
7. Is other people's acceptance and approval important to you?	[ ]	[ ]
8. Do you have a hard time liking yourself?	[ ]	[ ]
9. Do you permit abusive behavior from someone close to you, all the while allowing them to assume an influential role in your life?	[ ]	[ ]
10. Have you given away your power? Your Higher Power?	[ ]	[ ]

A Self-Test to Determine Whether Living With an Alcoholic Is Affecting Your Well-Being

	YES	NO
1. Were you ever afraid of being abused by the alcoholic in your life?	[ ]	[ ]
2. Do you often try to "fix" other people?	[ ]	[ ]
3. Do you feel isolated from friends because of secrets you must keep?	[ ]	[ ]
4. Do you have financial difficulties due to the alcoholic in your life?	[ ]	[ ]
5. Do you find it difficult to express your emotions?	[ ]	[ ]
6. Do you readily fulfill others' needs yet not your own?	[ ]	[ ]
7. Do you attract people who tend to be compulsive or abusive?	[ ]	[ ]
8. Do you recognize compulsive behavior in yourself?	[ ]	[ ]
9. Do you cling to relationships because you fear being alone?	[ ]	[ ]
10. Do you think a parent's drinking may have affected you?	[ ]	[ ]

A Self-Test for Compulsive Overworking

	YES	NO
1. Has work become your "drug of choice" for gaining approval from others?	[ ]	[ ]
2. Is work your favorite pastime and preferred topic of conversation?	[ ]	[ ]
3. Do you take on more work than you can successfully complete?	[ ]	[ ]
4. Have you ever lied about the amount of work you do?	[ ]	[ ]
5. Do you place unreasonable demands on yourself, often giving up weekends and vacations to complete projects?	[ ]	[ ]
6. Do you resent it when friends or family members fail to understand the importance of your professional commitments?	[ ]	[ ]
7. Are you chronically late for social engagements?	[ ]	[ ]
8. Do you have trouble meeting deadlines because you underestimate time requirements?	[ ]	[ ]
9. Do you sometimes fall asleep thinking about work?	[ ]	[ ]
10. Are you anxious about finances even in prosperous times?	[ ]	[ ]

A Self-Test to Determine Whether a Psychiatric Disorder in Conjunction with a Compulsive Behavior Is Affecting Your Well-Being

	YES	NO
1. Do you often regard your condition as hopeless?	[ ]	[ ]
2. Are you sometimes visited by voices that no one else hears?	[ ]	[ ]
3. Do you think other people tend to see you as "crazy"?	[ ]	[ ]
4. Have you ever lied to appear in better control of a situation?	[ ]	[ ]
5. Do you yearn for companionship and an opportunity to share some of your "weird" thoughts and feelings?	[ ]	[ ]
6. Do you tend to feel isolated and unable to communicate from your heart even in supportive settings?	[ ]	[ ]
7. Do you feel that no one understands you?	[ ]	[ ]
8. Are you fairly certain that "God stuff" will not work for you?	[ ]	[ ]
9. Are you increasingly dependent on medically prescribed drugs?	[ ]	[ ]
10. Do you long for relief from the chaos in your inner and outer worlds?	[ ]	[ ]

A Self-Test for the Compulsive Use of Nicotine

	YES	NO
1. Do you find that smoking helps you deal with stress?	[ ]	[ ]
2. Do you smoke when you first wake up in the morning and when you go to bed at night?	[ ]	[ ]
3. When you have the urge to smoke, do you find it difficult to concentrate on anything else?	[ ]	[ ]
4. Have you ever quit smoking? More than once?	[ ]	[ ]
5. Is it important to keep from running out of cigarettes?	[ ]	[ ]
6. Do you dislike other people telling you when or where to smoke?	[ ]	[ ]
7. Do you remember how you felt the first time you ever smoked?	[ ]	[ ]
8. Do you consider tobacco a good friend?	[ ]	[ ]
9. Has a physician ever advised you to quit smoking?	[ ]	[ ]
10. Would the quality of your life improve if you quit smoking?	[ ]	[ ]

Support Groups to Contact

The following support groups base their work on AA's Twelve-Step approach to sobriety, although certain Steps are slightly modified to address different behaviors. Sponsorship, too, is vital to each program, as is recognition for goals accomplished, in the form of a special chip, a medal, or acknowledgment from the membership.

To find meetings in your area, contact the appropriate group or check the phone book, search the Internet, or call your local church or AA office. Most of these resources are equipped to give you information on recovery from other addictions as well.

AA World Services, Inc.
PO Box 459
Grand Central Station
New York, NY 10163
212-870-3400

Cocaine Anonymous World Service Organization, Inc.
PO Box 492000
Los Angeles, CA 90049-8000
310-216-4444

Overeaters Anonymous
World Service Office
PO Box 44020
Rio Rancho, NM 87174-4020
505-891-2664

Sex and Love Addicts Anonymous
Fellowship-Wide Services, Inc.
PO Box 338
Norwood, MA 02062-0338
781-255-8825

Gamblers Anonymous International Service Office
PO Box 17173
Los Angeles, CA 90017
213-386-8789

Narcotics Anonymous World Services, Inc.
PO Box 9999
Van Nuys, CA 91409
818-773-9999

Debtors Anonymous General Services Board
PO Box 920888
Needham, MA 02492-0009
781-453-2743

National Council on Codependence, Inc.
PO Box 40095
Phoenix, AZ 85067-0095
602-735-6870

Al-Anon Family Group Headquarters, Inc.
1600 Corporate Landing Parkway
Virginia Beach, VA 23454-1655
757-563-1600

Workaholics Anonymous World Service Organization
PO Box 289
Menlo Park, CA 94026-0289
510- 273-9253

Double Trouble in Recovery
PO Box 245409
Brooklyn, NY 11224
718-996-6324

Nicotine Anonymous
PO Box 591777
San Francisco, CA 94159-1777
415-750-0328

Recommended Reading

Alcoholics Anonymous World Services, Inc. *Alcoholics Anonymous: The Story of How Many Thousands of Men and Women Have Recovered from Alcoholism* (The "AA Big Book"). New York: Alcoholics Anonymous World Services, 1939.

Alcoholics Anonymous World Services, Inc. *Pass It On: The Story of Bill Wilson and How the AA Message Reached the World.* New York: Alcoholics Anonymous World Services, 1984.

Das, Bhagavan. *The Essential Unity of All Religions.* Wheaton, IL: The Theosophical Press, 1932.

The Essential Rumi, trans. by Coleman Barks. New York: HarperCollins, 1995.

Fox, Emmet. *The Sermon on the Mount: The Key to Success in Life.* New York: Harper & Row, 1934.

Gawain, Shakti. *Creative Visualization.* San Rafael, CA: New World Library, 1978.

Helmstetter, Shad. *Self-Talk Solutions.* New York: Pocket Books, 1990.

Hill, Napoleon. *Think and Grow Rich.* New York: Ballantine, 1960.

Jung, C. G. *The Archetypes and the Collective Unconscious,* trans. by R. F. C. Hull. In *The Collected Works 9,* pt. 1, 2nd ed. Bollingen Series XX. Princeton, NJ: Princeton University Press, 1968.

Millman, Dan. *The Way of the Peaceful Warrior.* Emeryville, CA: H. J. Kramer, 1980.

Walsch, Neale Donald. *Conversations with God: An Uncommon Dialogue,* bk. 1. New York: Putnam Publishing Group, 1996; *Conversations with God,* bks. 2 and 3. Charlottesville, VA: Hampton Roads Publishing Company, 1997, 1998.

Williamson. Marianne. *Illuminata: A Return to Prayer.* New York: Berkley Publishing Group, 1995.

Yogananda, Paramahansa. *Autobiography of a Yogi.* Nevada City, CA: Crystal Clarity Publishers, 1994.

About the Author

Hob discovered his capacity to receive and record "inspired" thoughts at age thirteen, three years after the death of his father. Even while serving as a Marine Corps platoon sergeant during World War II, he found time to devote to writing. While employed as an advertising executive on Madison Avenue, however, he spiraled downward through a booze-laden "work ethic" and an alcoholic marriage.

In 1950 Hob quit his job in advertising and, still an "enthusiastic drinker," joined the United World Federalists' efforts to seek global peace. There, together with Oscar Hammerstein, Norman Cousins, John Hershey, and others, he created the magazine *One World or None* and coined the phrase "Peace is a fighting word"—a slogan that soon appeared in *The New York Times* as well as on banners across the country. All this time his inspired writing lay dormant.

Many jobs later, he overcame his denial about drinking and began a Twelve-Step return to sobriety, which helped him reclaim long-lost pieces of himself, including his inner voice. At this point "Hob"—a childhood nickname derived from his custom of traipsing around in his father's hob-nailed boots—came to mean "Hob **or b**ooze." And Hob it remained as he addressed numerous audiences and assisted dozens of people, including two of his own children, on the path to recovery. Now eighty-one years old and about to celebrate a twenty-one-year marriage to his fifth wife, Kairina, he is as dedicated as ever to awakening the power of love in people's lives.

Hob joined Alcoholics Anonymous on March 22, 1960, and has been sober ever since.

In a Hospital Waiting Room

The brain obeys the same laws
that make light move from a star
to the hospital room window
my old high school buddy and I
looked through last night
after his diagnostic procedure.

On TV we watched a show about cuneiform—
all those bills for sheep and property debts!
Somebody thousands of years ago
broke human speech into metaphors
that could be set in soft clay and figured out
long after their language died.

Then we remembered high school math and pi.
How hard the teachers must have worked
to make math and science dull.
Mr. Jones's first homework assignment:
Memorize the periodic table.
But Mr. Schwartz did try:
The distance around a perfect circle
will never—even after the end of time—
match up neatly with the distance through.

Maybe the brains that discovered pi,
And laws of light, and how to record debt
can help us figure out what's wrong.
And if not, we decided, we should at least find solace
in remembering that pi goes on forever.
But then he asked, where? Where does pi go on forever?

Advance praise for

Honoring Your Self...

"In *Honoring Your Self,* Hob leads the reader from denial and self-absorption to self-acceptance, self-forgiveness, and self-sharing. Hob's words inspire, comfort, and guide those on the path to recovery."

—JOHN BRADSHAW
Bestselling author of *Homecoming, Family Secrets,* and *Creating Love*

"*Honoring Your Self* is an excellent tool for personal transformation. Anyone can break the cycle of addiction and gain more personal freedom through the insightful and practical information presented in this book."

—DON MIGUEL RUIZ
Author of the Toltec Wisdom books
The Four Agreements and *The Mastery of Love*

"*Read this book.* Slowly. Thoughtfully. Prayerfully. With pencil in hand, mark it up. Underline. Scribble in the margins. Don't lend it to anyone. Keep it within reach—preferably, on the bedside table—so you can go back to special passages again and again. Filled with insight and faith, help and hope, it may well become one of the five or six books you value the most."

—WHITMAN HOBBS
Author, retired advertising executive, and
Former voice of the *New Yorker*

"For those who would like to awaken their soul while moving beyond the danger of addiction, the path suggested by Hob is a must. To know these Twelve Steps, the only step that is needed is to read this book."

—SUNIL V. JOSHI, MD (AYU)
Faculty advisor to The Chopra Center for Well Being
Author of *Ayurveda and Panchakarma: The Science of Healing and Rejuvenation*

"The answer to all our problems is a shift in collective consciousness away from hate, greed, and fear toward love, cooperation, and oneness. In his wonderfully inspiring and entertaining book, *Honoring Your Self,* Hob not only helps us understand the power of our higher self but moves us to reach for it."

—DENNIS WEAVER
Actor, and founder and president of the Institute of Ecolonomics